SPEAK
AMERICAN

A Survival Guide to the Language and Culture of the U.S.A.

By Dileri Borunda Johnston

Random House
New York

Speak American: A Survival Guide to the Language and Culture of the U.S.A.

Copyright © 2000 Random House, Inc.

This book is available for special purchases in bulk by organizations and institutions, not for resale, at special discounts. Please direct your sales inquiries to Random House Premium Sales, toll-free 800-800-3246 or fax 212-572-4961.

Please address inquiries about electronic licensing of reference products, for use on a network or in software or on CD-ROM, to the Subsidiary Rights Department, Random House Reference, fax 212-940-7352.

Visit the Random House Reference Web site: www.randomwords.com

Typeset and printed in the United States of America.

Library of Congress CIP Data is available.

First Edition
0 9
June 2002

ISBN 0-375-70468-X

Contents

Foreword

I figured I had the whole British English thing sussed when I arrived in London as a newlywed. After all, I had grown up reading *The Chronicles of Narnia* and *The Railway Children,* and watching *Brideshead Revisited* on PBS. I knew all about lifts and lorries and scones. So you can imagine my surprise the first time I walked into a sandwich bar and asked for a chicken salad sandwich. Instead of what I expected, I was given a few slices of chicken, lettuce, tomatoes, and bizarrely, cucumbers. It then became obvious that although I spoke English, I didn't necessarily speak the same language.

Speak American is for everyone who might have the same experience when visiting the U.S.A., or when working with American colleagues. It's for English speakers from Europe, Africa, India, Asia, Australia—whether native speakers or second language learners of English—who have been taught British English and have discovered that this does not mean they are prepared for American English.

Speak American is also more than a list of vocabulary words that are different, although we cover those thoroughly. We give advice on where to shop for certain things, how to tip service people, and how to phrase requests and questions so that you get what you want. Every chapter begins with a summary of confusable terms—British English terms that may mean something different in American English—Americanisms, grammar, and culture, so you can get the key information you need at a glance. A wealth of details and helpful hints follow the key points, and a glossary of terms ends each chapter.

Words in **dark type** in the chapters are defined in each glossary or in the text, along with many other words that you may need to know. British English equivalents are in *italic type* in these glossaries. The symbol ⇨ tells you where to look for more information in the book.

With this book in hand, you should feel confident in your ability to communicate with Americans. One word of warning, however: never, ever tell an American "you must visit if you're ever in my country" if you're only trying to be polite. An American will probably do it.

Chapter One
The Basics

Every English speaker in the world is aware of the American influence on the English vocabulary. You probably know many American terms from films, television programs, and pop music. You probably also know that Americans tend to use language that is direct and straightforward, and that many British idioms have no direct equivalent in American English. But what speakers of all "Englishes" usually don't know is how subtle the differences can be, and that many of these differences have to do with grammar.

We're about to describe the most basic differences in the structure of American grammar, spelling, and phrasing. In most cases, it's vocabulary differences that can actually cause you embarrassment, so if you can't be bothered with grammar, you can skip to Chapter Two.

However, if you want to be aware of why you may be getting a blank look from an American you're talking to, read on. Also, you'd do well to check the warnings labeled Big Mistake.

Little Differences Everywhere

Even when it comes to the simplest phrases, Americans put things just a little differently. For example:

Americans say:	**Americans *do not* say:**
Speaking of which . . .	*Talking of which . . .*
What's her name?	*What is she called?*
Do you have a pen?	*Have you got a pen?*
I'm going to take a bath.	*I'm going to have a bath.*
My keys are missing.	*My keys have gone missing.*
She had just gotten a new car.	*She had just got a new car.*
Wake me up at seven, please.	*Knock me up at seven, will you?*

Two big mistakes and one caution:

> **! Big Mistake:** In American English, to "knock someone up" means "to get a woman pregnant" and has nothing to do with waking someone up.
>
> **! Big Mistake:** If you say "She had just got a new car," an American will think you're not very well educated, for the simple reason that "gotten" is still the past participle of "get" in American English.
>
> **! Caution:** Americans prefer "have" to "have got" to show possession of something. If you say, "Have you got a pen?" Americans are likely to respond, "No, I don't" instead of "No, I haven't," because they are used to responding to questions that begin, "Do you have . . . ?"

Prepositions

If there is one thing that distinguishes speakers of American English from speakers of British English, it would have to be the use of prepositions. There are differences not only in the choice of preposition, but also in whether a preposition is used at all.

Americans say:	**Americans do not say:**
Susie fell down.	Susie fell over.
Drain the pasta.	Drain off the pasta.
He's always moving around.	He's always moving about.
They don't get along very well.	They don't get on very well.
an all-around great athlete	an all-round great athlete
Guess who came over today?	Guess who came round today?
That's different from what he said.	That's different to what he said.
Can't you stop him from going?	Can't you stop him going?
Please help me do this.	Please help me to do this.
I have to write (to) John this week.	I have to write to John this week.
Send it by mail.	Send it through the mail.
We got it in the mail.	We got it through the mail.
I used to wait (on) tables.	I used to wait at tables.
Jill was asking about you.	Jill was asking after you.

The Definite Article

The use of the definite article is another big difference between American and British English:

Americans say:
She's in the hospital.
In the future, please talk to me first.
It worked perfectly the first time.

Americans *do not* say:
She's in hospital.
In future, please talk to me first.
It worked perfectly first time.

In the Past

American English tends to use the simple past tense, whereas British English prefers the imperfect and the present perfect tenses. This does not mean that these other tenses are never used by Americans, but their use is usually limited to talking about actions that are finished by a specific time in the past.

Americans say:
She soon realized the truth.
We had a great time.
Did you bring the book?
Did you see my glasses?

Americans *do not* say:
She had soon realized the truth.
We've had a great time.
Have you brought the book?
Have you seen my glasses?

However, Americans say: *I had just turned seventeen when we met.*

Negatives

Americans usually put negative contractions in the helping verb in a sentence rather than contracting the helping verb with the pronoun:

Americans say:
I haven't seen her in ages.
We hadn't been there before.
I don't have a thing to wear.

Americans *do not* say:
I've not seen her in ages.
We'd not been there before.
I've not got a thing to wear.

Verbs

Americans use verbs that express the action instead of using a singular noun to describe an action that is performed:

Americans say:

Oh, you frightened me!
I'll talk to him tomorrow.
We slept in on Sunday.
I'd like to wash up before we eat.

Americans *do not* say:

Oh, you gave me a fright!
I'll have a word to him tomorrow.
We had a lie-in on Sunday.
I'd like to have a wash before we eat.

> **! Big Mistake:** To "wash up" in American English means to wash your face and hands, not to wash the dishes. If you offer to help someone wash up, that person had better be a child.

Get, Go, and Turn

Where British English uses "go" with adjectives to describe transitions, American English tends to use "get" or "turn":

Americans say:

Your dinner's getting cold.
The weather's turning cold.
The milk's turned sour.

Americans *do not* say:

Your dinner's going cold.
The weather's gone a bit cold.
The milk's gone off.

However, Americans say:

The meat's gone bad.

Americans *do not* say:

The meat's gone off.

Modals and Reckonings

Americans use *should* and *will* instead of *shall*, and *shouldn't* instead of *mustn't*, yet they use *would* where British English would use *should*:

Americans say:	**Americans do not say:**
Let's go now.	*Shall we go now?*
Should we go now?	
I'll have to ask her.	*I shall have to ask her.*
You shouldn't do that.	*You mustn't do that.*
Don't do that.	
I wouldn't be surprised if . . .	*I shouldn't wonder if . . .*

However, Americans say:	**Americans do not say:**
They demanded that she pay immediately.	*They demanded that she should pay immediately.*
I imagine that will be all right.	*I should imagine that will be all right.*

> ❗ **Caution:** *In American English, if you say* I reckon, *you will sound like you are trying to imitate a cowboy. Use* I figure *or* I think/guess/imagine.
>
> ❗ **Caution:** *Americans never say* needn't. *They say* don't have to: *You* don't have to *shout!*

The Fix Problem

Americans don't use *fix* to mean *attach*. They use *stick, put, attach, fasten, hang,* or *secure,* but nothing is ever *fixed to* something else.

Instead, Americans use *fix* where British English would use *mend: Can you fix my bike?* Only clothes and things made from fabric are *mended.*

Nouns

In American English, collective nouns usually take a singular verb, unless the members of a group are being spoken about as individuals:

Americans say:

*The new government is very
unpopular.*

*My family is going to Europe this
summer.*

*Ford is bringing out the new
models soon.*

Americans *do not* say:

*The new government are very
unpopular.*

*My family are going to Europe this
summer.*

*Ford are bringing out the new
models soon.*

> ❗ **Big Mistake:** Using a plural verb with a collective noun is another
> thing that will make you sound uneducated to an American.

Dates and Times

When writing or saying a date, Americans always put it
month/day/year, with a comma separating the day from the
year:

September 12, 2001
9/12/01

The time is written with a colon between the hour and the
minutes: 11:59. Americans do not use a 24-hour clock, even for
travel schedules. The only ones who will understand you if you
use "16:30" to mean "4:30" are people in the military.

In spoken American English, there are certain preferences
when telling time:

Americans say:

It's six-thirty./It's half past six.
Do you have the time?
What time do you have?

Americans *do not* say:

It's half six.
Have you got the time?
What time do you make it?

Americans *can* say:

*I'll see you at (a) quarter after
three.*

Americans can also use either "to" or "of" with "quarter": *She left at a quarter to eight.* In general, Americans say "a quarter to/after" rather than "quarter to/after" and "five-thirty" rather than "half past five." In general, they also prefer *What time is it?* to *What's the time?*

Farther and Further

Americans tend to be more careful about the use of these two words—or at least they have the feeling they *ought* to be more careful. "Farther" is usually used when talking about physical distances: *The grocery store is farther than the mall.* "Further" refers to matters of time, amount, or degree: *The police looked further into his past.*

Punctuation

Some easily confusable punctuation marks:

period: *a full stop*
quotation marks/quotes: *inverted commas*
exclamation point: *an exclamation mark*
parentheses: *brackets*
brackets: *square brackets*

You will have noticed already that we are using double quotes (" ") everywhere that you would expect to see single quotes. If you reverse the rule in British English, you have the American rule: double quotes surround quotations, and quotations inside quotations get single quotes: *Jan said, "My mother always told me, 'Never trust a stranger.'"* Also, commas and periods go inside the quotation marks rather than outside them.

Americans use "period" as an idiom in the same way "full stop" can be used: "What do you mean she was quiet? She didn't talk, period!"

Spelling

Rather than listing each and every little spelling variant between American and British English, we decided to list some of the most common differences:

Words spelled with "-ou-" lose the "u" in American English:

> *favorite*
>
> *color*
>
> *moldy*

Note that this does not apply to words that end in *"-ous"*: famous, marvelous.

Words that end in "-re" become "-er" in American English:

> *center*
>
> *theater*
>
> *meter*
>
> *caliber*

Words that end in "-ise" or "-yse"(and their derivatives) are usually spelled with a "z" in American English:

> *realize*
>
> *memorize*
>
> *organization*
>
> *analyze*

Many words spelled with a double consonant are spelled with just one in American English:

> *traveled*
>
> *worshiped*
>
> *jewelry*
>
> *grueling*
>
> *filet*

Just to confuse things, some words that are spelled with a single consonant have a double consonant in American English (which is why you should buy an American dictionary):

> *enrollment*
> *fulfill*

Words spelled with "ae" and "oe" are usually spelled with just the "e" in American English:

> *esophagus*
> *hemophilia*
> *leukemia*
> *esthetic*

Verbs whose past participle is spelled with a final "t" are usually spelled with "ed" in American English:

> *dreamed*
> *spilled*
> *learned*
> *burned*
> *spelled*

There's an exception to every rule, in this case: wept, crept, kept, slept. *Again, buy a dictionary that lists the irregular verb forms.*

Hyphenated words tend to be closed up in American English:

> *cooperate*
> *nontoxic*
> *southwest*
> *halftime*
> *mapmaking*
> *masklike*

Similarly, terms that are written as two words can be closed up in American English (have you bought that dictionary yet?):

> *anymore*
> *forever*

Words that indicate direction and end in "-wards" are usually written "-ward" in American English, although both endings are used when speaking:

> *forward*
> *toward*
> *backward*
> *afterward*

Abbreviations are written with a period after them:

> *Mr./Mrs./Ms.*
> *St. Louis*
> *Mt. Etna*

Except in legal citations, "versus" is abbreviated as *vs.*, not *v.*

Chapter Two
American Society

⚬⚏ Key Confusables:

British	American
cheers	= *only used in a toast, not to say "thanks"*
mate	= *friend*
working class	= *blue-collar*

⚬⚏ Key Americanisms:

Americans always say something when someone thanks them. "You're welcome" is the most common response.

If they bump into someone, or need to get past someone in a tight space, Americans say "Excuse me" rather than "Sorry."

Americans say:

"Thank you." "You're welcome."
"How are you?" "Fine, thanks."
"Excuse me, ma'am."
"Thanks."

Americans *do not* say:

"Thank you." "Cheers."
"How are you?" "Oh, not too bad."
"Excuse me, madam."
"Ta."

⚬⚏ Key Grammar:

In speech, Americans avoid using "he/him" to mean "any person, male or female." Instead, they use *they* as a singular noun: *"If anyone wants more soda, they can help themselves."* In formal writing, they use "he or she": *"If anyone wants more soda, he or she can help him or herself."* Because this sounds awkward, they will usually reword the sentence: *"Anyone who wants more soda can get it from the fridge."* You'll notice that we're using "they" as a singular noun in this book, because we think it's easier.

You will often hear Americans use the adjectives *good* and *real* rather than the adverbs *well* and *really*: *"How are you?" "Real good, thanks."*

⚬⚏ Key Cultural Points:

Americans are generally very polite. You'll often hear "please," "thank you," and "excuse me." However, they tend not to apologize as much as people seem to do in other countries, and they like positive statements better than negative ones: *"The weather's nice today"* rather than *"The weather's not bad today."* "Sir" and "Ma'am" are commonly used when speaking to strangers.

Americans try to be direct and honest when dealing with others. They are also open and friendly, even if they do not intend to start a friendship with someone.

....

Classless Society

The United States society is not truly classless, but don't tell an American that. It's true that it does not have the same centuries-old class divisions that exist in many other countries. Instead, it has a remarkably mobile society that rewards and admires anyone who is able to succeed, especially if success involves making a lot of money.

While there is a long-established class of white people of Anglo-Saxon origin, or **WASPs,** who have traditionally held wealth and power in the country, there are equally rich and powerful people from other ethnic backgrounds. There is a more marked division between **blue-** and **white-collar** workers, which extends into most areas of people's lives, from where they live to what they do in their spare time. Some activities, such as bowling and playing pool, are seen as blue-collar, and other ones, such as golfing and going to the opera, are seen as white-collar.

It is generally money rather than family background that marks the difference in classes in the U.S., except for a fairly small social circle in the Northeast.

Talk, Talk, Talk

To people from other countries, Americans may seem loud and embarrassing to be with, and too willing to share their entire life stories with strangers. To Americans, however, that is considered normal, friendly behavior. What does confuse newcomers to the United States is that although an American may have shared some very private information with them, it does not necessarily lead to a long and lasting friendship. Openness and honesty are just part of the American character, and any reserve or shyness on the part of strangers may be taken as snobbishness, or a sign that they may have something to hide.

Business Relations

When it comes to doing business, Americans are generally quite informal and relaxed in their relations with people, but they are very, very serious about business itself. Most people who work together call each other by their first names, including the **CEO.**

When meeting someone for the first time, it is best to wait for them to ask to be called by their first name. Until then, it is probably best to call them by their title and their surname.

Americans tend to be friendly and polite in their business dealings, but the bottom line is that it is still business, no matter how friendly. They are also very honest and up-front, and will not hesitate to say what needs to be said. To some people it may seem very direct and even rude, but if something is not happening the way it should, Americans will speak up and expect the person they are dealing with to do something about it. In the opposite situation, if someone has done a job particularly well, an American business associate will be eager to praise that person.

Business Letters

Unless you know the person you are writing to very well, use a title and the person's last name when you begin a letter:

Dear Ms. Jones,
Dear Dr. Brown,

Always use *Ms.* for a woman unless you know that she prefers *Mrs.* or *Miss.* If you can't tell from the name whether the person is a man or a woman, it is acceptable to use the person's full name in the greeting, although it's better to find out their sex first:

Dear Terry Carlson,

Terry Carlson, if he's at all aware of the problem, should sign his name *Mr. Terry Carlson* when he responds to you, to end the confusion. Americans don't usually use the British method of *Terry Carlson (Mr.),* but it's a nice solution.

If you don't know the name of the person you are writing to, for example because you are writing to a company to complain about something, use "Dear Sir or Madam":

Dear Sir or Madam:

I am writing to complain about the service I received in your restaurant yesterday.

If you are responding to a letter that someone sent, start by thanking them:

Dear Mr. Johnson,

Thank you for your letter of July 1.

When ending a business letter, close with "Yours truly" or "Yours sincerely":

Yours truly,

Alan Parks

If you started your letter with "Dear Sir or Madam," you are supposed to use "Yours faithfully," but most Americans don't—they still use "Yours sincerely," or just "Sincerely" if they want to seem very serious or slightly angry.

Direct Is Best

Americans do not understand people who seem to be friendly and say "yes" a lot just because it is expected in a business situation. If you are friendly, seem to agree about many things, and business discussions have gone well, Americans will think that you have reached an agreement. If you then go back to your country and decide that you cannot agree to certain points after all, an American will feel betrayed. Americans are more comfortable with conflict, and even outright aggression, than they are with what they see as dishonesty.

The general American attitude to work and to any problems that arise at work is a confident, we-can-do-it spirit, and they generally expect this same attitude from anyone they work with. The American workplace is also highly competitive, an attitude that is encouraged early on in children and young people through the competitive nature of American schools, sports, and other activities.

Touchy, Touchy

If you think about it, it's logical that since Americans like being direct and honest, they don't like jokes that insult people. In other cultures, mild insults are just part of social joking; in the United States, people take such comments seriously and get offended. They do not like to be embarrassed in public, so don't play any jokes on anyone unless you know that person very, very well.

Have a Nice Day

Most people who work in the service industries (restaurants, hotels, shops) are expected to do their jobs with a positive and friendly attitude. This may come across as somewhat false to some people, who find all those cheery "Hi, theres" and "Have a nice days" a bit annoying. But it is better than getting service with a snarl. Even when working at a **Mcjob**, Americans are expected to do their job as well as possible, and pride is taken in providing pleasant service to customers. Americans will complain to managers or not tip well if service has not been friendly.

Marriage and Family

There is no law in the United States about how many children a couple can have, whether a woman must take her husband's name (although a majority still do), or what names children are allowed to have. The average number of children comes out to 2.4, and you will sometimes hear "a couple with 2.4 children" used to mean "the average family." Many women hyphenate their last names when they marry, so that if Susan Smith marries Bill Jones, she becomes Susan Smith-Jones. Their children, however, usually have the father's last name.

Families are modern and complicated in the United States; the divorce rate is one out of two marriages, so there are a lot of families with only one parent or with stepparents. Women usually work at least part-time outside the home, and so many children who are too young for school spend all or part of their days in **day care.** Families still try to eat their evening meal together at home, but this is often not possible because of parents' work schedules or children's after-school activities. (⇨ *High School* on page 114)

Many couples now live together without being married, or live together for a period of time before they marry. Adults in these relationships sometimes prefer the word **partner** to the words "boyfriend" or "girlfriend." Homosexual couples with children are increasingly common, although mostly in large cities where people tend to be a little more tolerant.

Americans say **Mom** *and* **Mommy,** *not "Mum" and "Mummy."*

Unmentionables

For all their willingness to talk about personal matters, there are a few subjects that Americans prefer not to discuss with anyone other than their closest friends and relatives. These topics are religion, money, and politics.

Religion

A newcomer to the United States can ask an American about religious customs in the country or the area where they live. It would, however, be very impolite to ask directly what their beliefs are. In fact, it seems like the only people who discuss their religious backgrounds at any length are stand-up comedians, who often build entire acts around how their family's religion has affected their lives.

Americans on the whole are fairly religious, and any religion that has ever existed on this planet will have at least a few followers in the United States. Christian groups are the most common, and conservative ones tend to be very active in politics. There is no official government religion; the separation of the church and the state is one of the basic principles of American government.

Money

When it comes to money, it is considered bad taste to ask someone how much they earn or how much they paid for something. Since Americans do love a bargain, they will sometimes volunteer how much something cost if they got it for a particularly good price.

> **! Warning:** *In some companies, you can lose your job if you tell a colleague what your salary is.*

Politics and Other No-nos

Many Americans do not like social arguments or heated discussions in the same way that some Europeans do. Therefore, it is not wise to bring up the subject of politics unless you are reasonably sure that your comments are generally in agreement with the beliefs of the other people present.

Americans may seem quite willing to discuss sexual matters and family problems with most people, judging by the huge number of revealing talk shows on television. Actually, the people who bare their souls on television shows are the exception rather than the rule. As in most countries, sex is a very personal matter and not usually a subject of conversation at dinner or at a party.

It is not polite to ask anyone other than a child how old they are.

Political Correctness

America is known as the land of political correctness—the practice of being very careful with your language to avoid offending anyone. Actually, most Americans think that a little sensitivity to issues of gender, race, and sexual orientation is a good idea, but that does not mean that they are watching every little thing they say.

Certain terms have, however, made their way into everyday American English and are now regarded as normal, rather than the "correct" but unusual way of saying something. This is probably most true of terms that substitute for words that are considered sexist; words such as "actor," "server," and "letter carrier" are used as commonly as "actress," "waitress," and "mailman."

People are also more careful when referring to Americans of nonwhite racial or ethnic origin. Terms like *African-American, Asian-American,* and *Mexican-American* are now frequently used. And rather than refer to someone as being "handicapped," it is best to say they "have a disability."

Profanity

Americans tend to watch their language, especially when in business or other formal situations, although it is obvious from watching the average Hollywood movie that Americans can be pretty foul-mouthed when they want to be. So it is best to save more colorful language for more informal moments, when you feel reasonably confident that none of your listeners will be offended.

It is also worth keeping in mind that while most swear words are the same in all varieties of English, there are some differences between British and American English. For instance, Americans do not use the words "wanker," "tosser," "git," or "prat," opting instead for something like **jerk** or "asshole."

> **! Warning:** *Be careful not to confuse the meaning of the word fanny, which in American English is a polite, old-fashioned term for someone's buttocks. And yes, those bags that can be strapped around the waist for carrying wallets, passports, and cameras are actually called fanny packs. Bum is not used in this sense. Another word that may cause confusion and offense is the word fag, which is a derogatory term for a homosexual, rather than slang for a cigarette. The variant faggot is equally offensive.*

Other terms that are likely to get strange looks in the United States are "bollocks," "sod off," and "shag," although the latter may make it into common usage after featuring prominently in the *Austin Powers* movies.

When expressing disapproval or dislike of something, Americans do not use the following words or construction: "That was a shit/crap/shite movie." Instead, they are more likely to say something to the effect of "That was a really shitty/crappy/bad movie." or "That movie really **sucked.***"*

Yankees

Outside of the United States, all Americans get called Yankees. Inside the United States, however, it's a different story. A Yankee is someone who comes from one of the northern states that fought for the Union against the southern Confederates, in the war that northerners call the Civil War and that southerners call the War Between the States. In the South, a Yankee can also be anyone who isn't from the South, although westerners argue that they can't be called Yankees since most of their states didn't even exist in the 1860s when the war took place. And in the Northeast, only someone from New England is a Yankee.

Feelings about that war are still very strong in the South, so it's best never to bring up the subject.

· ·

Glossary of American Terms

Asian

In the United States, the term "Asian" is used to refer to someone or something from China, Japan, Korea, the Philippines, or Southeast Asia. While India is part of Asia, its people tend to be called "people from India" or "Indian Indians" (as opposed to American Indians).

blue-collar

the class of workers whose jobs involve manual work and usually require uniforms or less formal clothing.

CEO

chief executive officer; the person with the most authority in a company; *managing director.*

day care

a building or home where very young children are taken care of while their parents are at work.

hyphenated American

someone whose family did not come from northern Europe and is called by their ethnic background, such as Asian-American,

African-American, Latino-American. This term is a little negative; it is better to say "minorities" or "ethnic Americans."

Indian
someone or something from India. ⇨ *Native American.*

JAP
Jewish American Princess; an offensive term for a girl from a
well-to-do Jewish family. In the same way, BAP means Black
American Princess.

jerk
a stupid or annoying person.

Mcjob
a low-paid job in a service industry.

Native American
The terms "Native American" or "American Indian" are now
used when talking about one of the indigenous peoples of the
Americas, although some Native Americans use the term
Indian as a point of pride and identity when talking about
themselves.

suck
to be of very bad quality.

WASP
White Anglo-Saxon Protestant; used to refer to a person who
comes from this background, which has traditionally made up
the upper classes in the United States.

white-collar
the class of workers whose jobs do not involve manual work and
usually require business clothing such as suits.

Chapter Three
Eating and Drinking

🔑 *Key Confusables:*

British	American
bill	= *check*
biscuit	= *cookie*
canteen	= *cafeteria*
crêpes	= *pancakes**
crisps	= *chips*
cutlery	= *silverware/flatware*
electric whisk	= *mixer*
fish slice	= *spatula*
grill	= *broiler*
jug	= *pitcher*
liquidiser	= *blender*
main (course)	= *entrée*
pudding/sweet	= *dessert*
starter	= *appetizer*
sweets	= *candy*
a take-away	= *a takeout*
tin	= *can*
white coffee	= *coffee with milk or cream*

*Pancakes in the United States are thick and nothing like the French-style pancakes that are still called "crepes" in America.

EATING & DRINKING

🔑 *Key Americanism:*

Americans usually say "go out for breakfast/lunch/dinner" rather than "go out for a meal."

🔑 *Key Grammar:*

Americans tend to think of most foods and drinks as uncountable nouns, so, for example, they would drink "some coffee," rather than "a coffee."

Americans say:	**Americans *do not* say:**
Let's get some ice cream.	*Let's get an ice cream.*
They make the best pizza in town.	*They make the best pizzas in town.*
I got a takeout salad for lunch.	*I had a takeaway for lunch.*
Would you like that for here or to go?	*Is that to eat in or take away?*
I'd like lettuce and tomatoes on my sandwich, please.	*I'll have salad on that sandwich, please.*
Do you want some mashed potatoes?	*Do you want some mash?*

EATING & DRINKING

⚷ Key Cultural Point:

Americans are very specific when ordering food and will not hesitate to complain or send food back if they don't get what they want. This is not considered rude.

Why Such a Big Chapter About Food?

Well, quite simply, because the biggest differences in vocabulary and customs seem to be connected to eating and drinking. After all, if you're in America, you'll be dealing with this three times a day or more, so we thought it was best to start with the thing you'll encounter most often.

Eating Out

Americans eat out frequently, because it is generally affordable and convenient. Most American cities have a wide range of eating options, from well-known fast-food joints to all-you-can-eat buffets, to specialty and ethnic restaurants. While specialty restaurants are much more common in larger cities, even smaller cities have at least an Italian, a Chinese, or a Mexican restaurant. But influences from other cultures have made their way into everyday American eating habits, too.

Melting Pot Menus

The French influence: Let's face it. The French defined *haute cuisine* ("high cooking"—a word you'll read in restaurant reviews), and the American restaurant experience still owes a lot to the French. This is clear when looking at the vocabulary used in restaurants and on menus.

Head waiters are often referred to as **maître d's,** although the full "maître d'hôtel" is not used very much. The wine steward is sometimes called the **sommelier.** This is the case in more expensive places. But French terms are also common on menus in less expensive restaurants, such as **entrée** (although Americans use this to mean "main course"), **à la carte** (= individually priced items), and many sauces and cooking styles. In more expensive restaurants, you'll now find a **prix fixe** (= fixed price) **menu,** which Americans previously encountered only on vacation in Europe. It almost seems un-American to limit people's eating choices.

French isn't the only language found in American food talk. Italian, German, and Eastern European foods have been part of American culture for almost a century, and people are familiar with foods such as pasta, **schnitzel, bagels,** and **knishes.** More recent immigrants have introduced a whole new vocabulary to Americans, for example **tortillas, gyoza,** and **gyros.** You really need to just look at the item or ask a **server** (= waiter/waitress) to describe it to you.

Servers are usually happy to give you a full explanation of what's in a dish, but they may talk too quickly for you to understand it. It is perfectly acceptable to say "I'm sorry, could you say that again more slowly, please?"

Picky, Picky

Most Americans seem really picky about their food in restaurants. Many people are on diets, or have allergies to food, so they will order their coffee with **2% milk,** their bagel with **non-fat** cream cheese, or their salad with the dressing **on the side.**

Most eating establishments are happy to make changes or substitutions. There may be a small charge for a substitution.

Ordering food in an American restaurant may be something of an ordeal to someone new to the experience. Diners are always faced with a lot of questions. Main courses usually come with vegetables and rice or potatoes, so you will be asked, "Soup or salad?" "Baked potato, fries, or rice?" "What dressing would you like with that? **Italian**, blue cheese, **French**, **ranch**, honey mustard?" The list can be endless.

Breakfast is probably the most daunting meal in terms of making decisions, and probably best avoided by anyone who can't make decisions early in the morning. It may seem simple enough to order eggs and bacon, but in America, it's not quite that straightforward. Eggs can be scrambled, fried, **over easy, sunnyside up**, poached, **soft-boiled**, or any other number of variations. Then there's the matter of bread—white, wholewheat, rye, bagel, muffin, tortilla.

Americans think they are not getting what they pay for unless they get huge amounts of food. So be warned: it is easy to order too much. This is where the **doggy bag** *comes in—many people ask for any leftover food to be wrapped up or boxed so they can take it away to finish later. This is not only normal, it's expected!*

Generally, though, Americans leave a big breakfast, or a big **brunch**, for the weekend, while weekday breakfasts are usually quick and informal, consisting of coffee, juice, and cereal or a **muffin** or other type of bread. Lunch, too, is quick, with sandwiches, soups, and salads being popular choices.

Dinner is the main meal of the day. Most people eat dinner fairly early, between about five o'clock and seven o'clock in the evening, but this can be later in big cities or when people are dining out.

Dinner *usually means the evening meal, but it is also used for the main meal of the day.* **Supper** *is always an evening meal and usually means an evening meal you eat at home. It is also used to mean a lighter evening meal if you ate a very large dinner at lunchtime, especially on Sundays, when the main meal is often at midday.*

Sandwiches and Salads

The sandwich may have been invented in England, but Americans turned sandwich-making into an art form. The ready-made, plastic-packed sandwich that you often get in Britain isn't really a concept in the United States. If you are having a sandwich for lunch, either you will have made it yourself at home or you will go to a restaurant or **deli** that makes sandwiches to order. Customers ordering sandwiches are very specific about how they want them prepared or **dressed.**

Mayonnaise and mustard are almost always spread on the bread in American sandwiches; Americans hardly ever put butter or margarine on sandwiches. If you ask for a sandwich with salad on it, Americans will not understand—you have to ask for "lettuce and tomato."

*Sandwiches are commonly served with **sweet** or **dill pickles**, but not with raw cucumbers. The substance called "pickle" in British English—the sweet and tangy sauce made in all kinds of ways—is called **relish** (if it is made from cucumbers) in the United States. Americans do usually know what chutney is, but they rarely eat it.*

The **salad bar** is another popular lunch option. Many restaurants and delis have salad bars, where customers can choose from a wide variety of vegetables and prepared salads—more than you have probably ever seen in your life.

Business Meals

Americans often schedule business meetings during meals. They do not wait until after the meal to discuss business: time is important, and it is not rude to talk about business during a meal. Breakfast meetings are scheduled early and do not last much more than an hour. Lunch is rarely more than one-and-a-half to two hours, and most Americans do not drink alcoholic beverages with their midday meal (⇨ **Drinking** on page 33). Evening meals or events tend to be more social, and having a few drinks is acceptable, but they also can end fairly early, since most people consider their personal time very important.

Who Pays?

If someone is invited for a meal, especially for business, the person who made the invitation will pay the **check.** Among friends, it is quite common in the United States for each person in a group to pay only for his or her part of the total. This practice is known as **going Dutch** or **splitting the check.** The check may be divided equally, or every person's own share of the total may be worked out. The American sense of fairness makes this quite acceptable—if you only had a salad, why pay for someone else's steak?—but in business, it is more polite to pay an equal share no matter what you ate.

Eating at Someone's Home

If you are invited to someone's home for dinner, the main thing to remember is to pretend to like the food even if you don't. It is perfectly acceptable to tell someone beforehand, "I'd love to come, but I'm a vegetarian; will that be a problem?" or to tell your host if you have any food allergies, but if the only reason you can't eat the food is that you don't like it, try to be polite and eat a couple of bites anyway, and ask for more of something you do like.

People usually bring flowers or wine to the host's house when they come for dinner; flowers are safer because people may not drink alcohol or may not share your taste in wine. Your host will probably open the bottle of wine you brought unless you say that it is "for you, for whenever you want." (The charming and useful expression "for the house" is not understood in the United States.)

If you like a particular dish, the best compliment you can give the cook is to ask for the recipe.

People usually eat "family style," putting plates and dishes of

EATING & DRINKING

food on the table for everyone to serve themselves from. Table manners may be a little more relaxed than in a restaurant, but you should be as polite as you can be even if some other guests are not.

When you leave, thank your host for the lovely time you had, and try to invite that person to the next dinner party at your own home if you are staying in the U.S. for a while. Some people write thank-you notes, although this is not expected.

Table Manners

There are a few rules that most Americans follow when eating, which can be different from customs in other countries:

- People usually wait for everyone to be served before they start eating; however, other diners may politely insist that the person who has been served start before the food gets cold.
- If your table has been served wine, wait until everyone has been served before you drink.
- Americans use their right hand to eat unless they are left-handed. If you cut something, set down your knife on your plate and put your fork in your right hand before you take a bite.
- Any hand that is not being used for eating should be kept in your lap. You can also rest a forearm on the edge of the table, but never put an elbow on the table.
- Put the knife and fork together on the plate to show the server that the plate can be removed.
- Do not drink from a bowl, or lift it off the table.
- Do not eat noisily.
- Keep your mouth closed when eating, and never talk with food in your mouth.
- If you have to burp, apologize by saying, "excuse me." Try not to burp at all.
- Do not smoke at a table unless you are sitting in the smoking section of a restaurant and everyone with you has finished eating.

EATING & DRINKING

Drinking

For the average American, drinking is very much something that is done outside of business. While alcohol is almost always a part of social situations, it is not the focus of an evening's entertainment. People often meet for drinks, but that is just the excuse for getting together and talking to friends or business associates. The amount that people drink has gone down quite a lot in recent years, and *it is not considered acceptable to drink at lunchtime on a workday.*

The basic American drinking establishment is the **bar**, although many other places are licensed to sell alcoholic beverages, such as restaurants, nightclubs, **taverns**, and most sports arenas. Depending on the type of bar, drinks are ordered either directly at the bar from the **bartender**, or from the server if there is table service. Since Americans are very fond of **cocktails**, most bartenders can mix most drinks.

EATING & DRINKING

Americans can be very strict about drinking alcohol, so this time we have not one, but two warnings:

❗ **1. Bring your passport.** *If you go to a bar, or buy alcohol in a store, bring identification with you that proves you are 21 or older. Even if you are old enough, if you look young and a bartender cards you or a store clerk asks for **ID** (identification), you must prove your age, or you will be told to leave the bar or will not be allowed to buy alcohol. The ID must have your picture and age on it.*

❗ **2. Don't drink and drive.** *Americans are very aware of drunk driving laws, but they do not count alcohol in units. The percentage of alcohol is not usually shown on drink containers. Every state in America has its own law about the percentage of alcohol it takes to be drunk, and the legal penalties can be very, very harsh, so the best thing to do is to not drink at all if you are going to drive. Some bars give free nonalcoholic drinks to **designated drivers** (people who don't drink alcohol so they can drive their friends home), so it is worth it to tell a bartender if you are the designated driver.*

In America, beer tends to have less alcohol in it than in other countries—usually around 4 percent. Bars usually have a small selection of **draft beers** as well as bottled beers, which are often called **longnecks.** Draft beer is served in glasses (about half a pint), in pints (which are smaller than British pints), or in pitchers (which contain four or five American pints). ⇨ **Weights and Measures** on page 185.

American beer used to be almost undrinkable. However, since the relatively recent development of the **microbrewery** and **brewpub,** beer can be very tasty, and worth trying. Another place to find a pint is in one of the Irish or English theme bars that are appearing around the country.

Nonalcoholic Drinks

Americans may not drink as many alcoholic beverages as people in other countries, but they more than make up for it with the number of **soft drinks** they consume. There are many regional differences when it comes to the term for soft drinks: **soda** in the Northeast, **pop** in the Midwest and West, and **cold drink** in the South. There is also an amazing variety of soft drinks available, and many have diet versions (without sugar).

Iced tea is also a very popular drink. Most restaurants will give you sugar and lemon to put in it, but in the South, it may already be very sweet.

Coffee is probably drunk more than any other drink in the United States, but unless you are in a large city, it will not be the strong European type (**espresso**). Americans tend to drink many cups of the weaker coffee that is made in electric coffee makers, all through the day. However, coffee shops with stronger drinks are becoming more popular all the time. These shops use the Italian words for types of coffee drinks: **latte** (espresso with milk), and **cappuccino** (espresso with milk and milk foam).

Hot tea is not a drink that Americans have very often. When they do, it is fairly bitter and weak, and they drink it with lemon and sugar rather than milk. Herbal teas, such as peppermint and chamomile, are fairly popular.

Americans do not understand the phrase "white coffee." American coffee is usually served with a small container of milk, cream, or **half-and-half***. Coffee without milk is called "black." If you ask for "regular" coffee in the Northeast, it will have milk or cream and sometimes sugar in it; in other places it will be black.*

Most restaurants will serve customers a glass of ice water as soon as they sit down, and they will refill it constantly throughout the meal without charge. Coffee is often refilled as often as you want as well.

Shopping for Food and Drinks

While there are specialized food shops in the United States, especially in larger cities, the majority of Americans shop for food at large supermarkets. These often have specialty areas inside them such as deli counters and bakeries. As with so many things in the United States, American supermarkets are usually very big. There will nearly always be someone at the **checkout counter** (where you pay for your food) to put your groceries in bags for you.

The following is a quick list of common foods that have different names in American English:

British	**American**
aubergine	*eggplant*
bap	*bun*
bicarbonate of soda	*baking soda*
biscuit	*cookie*
bolognaise sauce	*spaghetti sauce, meat sauce*
brown bread	*whole-wheat bread*
caster sugar	*granulated sugar, superfine sugar*
chickpea	*garbanzo bean (in the western United States)*
coriander	*cilantro, Chinese parsley*
cornflour	*cornstarch*

(continued)

EATING & DRINKING

British	American
Cos lettuce	*romaine lettuce*
courgette	*zucchini*
double cream	*heavy cream*
endive	*chicory, Belgian endive*
frisée	*endive*
haricots verts	*green beans*
jelly	*Jell-O™, gelatin*
joint	*roast*
kitchen roll	*paper towels*
mangetout	*snow peas*
marrow	*squash*
mince	*ground beef, hamburger*
mince pie	*mincemeat pie*
pitta bread	*pita bread*
plain chocolate	*bittersweet chocolate*
plain flour	*all-purpose flour*
prawns	*shrimp (always an uncountable noun)*
red/green pepper	*bell pepper*
rocket	*arugula*
self-raising flour	*self-rising flour*
single cream	*light cream*
sultanas	*golden raisins*
swede	*rutabaga*
Swiss roll	*jellyroll*
treacle	*molasses*

What you won't find in the United States: anything blackcurrant–flavored, and squash. If you want something close to blackcurrant, try grape juice (the purple kind), especially Concord grape juice. Squash is a gourd, not a concentrated drink, in the United States. Anything called a "fruit drink" (which means there's a lot of sugar in it, not just pure juice), will taste similar.

Soft drinks can be bought almost anywhere, but alcoholic drinks are another story. Every state has different rules about when and where you can buy alcohol, and it often depends on whether the alcohol is beer or wine, or **liquor.** People in New York buy beer, wine, and liquor only in special stores that are closed on Sundays. People in Washington can only buy liquor at a state-run liquor store, but they can buy beer and wine in supermarkets. Californians can buy all types of alcohol in a grocery store.

Bars also close at different hours of the night depending on the state you're in. And to top it off, in some states there are "dry counties"—counties where you can't buy any alcohol, anywhere, anytime, period. Needless to say, it's best to ask. In the state of Utah, you can't buy alcohol at all, unless you belong to a special club. At least the *names* for liquors are the same!

Cooking

The biggest thing you will notice about trying to cook in the United States is that you won't know how to measure anything. Americans use ounces, pounds, and pints rather than the metric system, of course (➡ **Weights and Measures** on page 185). But they also use special measuring containers that hold specific amounts of food, rather than weighing things like flour and sugar.

The containers come in cup sizes: for dry foods, you have 1 cup, 1/2 cup, 1/4 cup, and 1/8 cup, and for liquids, you have 2-cup or 4-cup containers. A cup is equal to 8 liquid ounces; butter comes in sticks that are equal to 1/2 cup each. Confused yet? If you will be staying in the United States long enough to need to cook and read recipes, you should buy a set of measuring cups and measuring spoons.

Cakes are baked in **baking pans**, *cookies and biscuits on* **cookie sheets**. *Use a* **mixer** *to mix the ingredients for a cake, and a* **blender** *for mixing and puréeing foods and liquids. Turn cooking food over with a* **spatula** *or a* **pancake turner**. *Food is cooked on* **stoves** *or* **ranges** *(➡ **Appliances and Electricity** on page 144), not on cookers, and ovens have* **broilers**, *not grills.*

Glossary of American Terms

1% milk
milk with one percent milk fat in it; another type of lowfat milk.

2% milk
milk with two percent milk fat in it; also known as lowfat milk; *semi-skimmed*.

à la mode
served with a scoop of ice cream on top, as in "apple pie à la mode."

all you can eat
All-you-can-eat restaurants charge a set price and allow customers to help themselves to as much food as they like, usually from a long counter or bar.

American cheese
a soft, orange food that is made with milk and that is meant to taste like cheese, although we don't think it does. It comes wrapped in individual slices and is used in sandwiches and hamburgers.

appetizer
the first course in a meal; *starter*.

bacon
What Americans call bacon is the smoked "streaky" type of bacon. It comes in slices, not rashers. ⇨ **Canadian bacon**.

bagel
a ring-shaped bread roll that is thick and chewy. Bagels are boiled briefly before being baked.

baked beans
beans cooked with tomato sauce and other seasonings. They are usually served as a side dish with barbecued foods. Americans don't usually eat them on toast or baked potatoes, and they never eat them with breakfast.

baked potato
a potato cooked whole and unpeeled in the oven; *jacket potato*.

baking chocolate
a type of very bitter chocolate, with no sugar in it, used in baking.

baking powder
a mixture of bicarbonate of soda and cream of tartar (don't ask—we don't know what this really is either). It is used instead of yeast to make biscuits light.

bar
a place that serves all kinds of alcoholic beverages, soft drinks, and sometimes snack foods. A bar is also an area inside a restaurant or other public place where alcoholic beverages are prepared and sold. Bars usually have a counter behind which the bartender stands and serves drinks.

barbecue
This word can be used for any type of meat that is cooked over an open fire. It usually means meat that has been cooked this way with a spicy tomato sauce. There are regional and state preferences for what type of meat is used and what the sauce is like. A barbecue is also a social event where food is cooked this way, or the object that is used for cooking it.

bartender
someone who works in a bar preparing and serving alcoholic drinks.

beef jerky
thin pieces of beef that are salted and dried to preserve them.

biscuit
a type of bread made with baking powder and baked in small rounds, often eaten at dinner. Think of a biscuit as a scone that is not sweet.

blender
an electric device for mixing, crushing, and puréeing foods and liquids; *liquidiser*.

bologna
a large, smoked sausage with a mild taste, made from a mixture of meats. It is usually sold in slices and eaten in sandwiches. It can also be spelled **baloney.**

Boston cream pie
not actually a pie, but a sponge cake filled with custard and covered with chocolate.

EATING & DRINKING

brewpub

a bar that brews its own beer to sell at that bar. It's also called a **microbrewery.**

broiler

the part of an oven (either at the top of the main oven or in a separate part underneath) used for cooking food quickly with direct heat. Do not call this a *grill*.

brownie

a moist, chewy chocolate cake.

brunch

a meal that is a cross between breakfast and lunch. People usually go out for brunch on the weekend, because it is a long, leisurely meal that involves a lot of different foods, including breakfast foods such as pancakes, waffles, and omelets along with meats and vegetables. Brunch may also include alcoholic beverages such as **mimosas.**

busboy

someone who takes away dirty dishes and silverware in a restaurant, sets tables, and helps the server. The term "busser" is also used because women do this job too.

buttermilk

thick, slightly sour-tasting milk with all the cream and fat still in it.

cafeteria

a place in a school, hospital, or office building where food is made and served; *canteen*. In cafeterias, customers choose their food from a serving line. The food served is usually very basic, and there are not many restaurants that are cafeterias.

cake pan

a round or square pan for baking cakes and breads in; *cake tin*.

can

a metal container for food and drinks; *tin*.

Canadian bacon

bacon made from the loin of a pig; *back bacon*. This is commonly found as a topping on pizza.

candy

sweet foods such as chocolate bars, peppermints, and toffee.

carry-out

another word for **takeout.**

case

a box containing 24 cans or bottles of beer, or 12 bottles of wine.

cereal

the name for any breakfast food eaten with milk, such as corn flakes, bran flakes, etc.

check

the piece of paper showing the total price of a meal in a restaurant; *bill.*

cheddar cheese

American cheddar cheese is usually orange. It varies in flavor from mild to very **sharp.**

chicken salad

a dish made with cooked chicken, celery, hard-boiled eggs, and mayonnaise. Often eaten in sandwiches.

chili dog

a hot dog topped with chili and sometimes cheese.

chips

thin round fried pieces of potato; *crisps.* Chips are also made from tortillas or a thicker corn mixture. The long thin pieces of fried potato are only called "chips" in the dish "fish and chips"; otherwise, they're **fries.**

cinnamon roll

a bun made of yeast dough that is spread with cinnamon, sugar, and butter, then rolled and baked.

cocktail

an alcholic drink such as vodka, gin, whiskey, mixed with juice, soda, or other ingredients.

coffee cake

a rich cake topped with a crumbly topping of sugar, butter, flour, cinnamon, and often nuts. The name comes from the fact that it is often served with coffee, not because it is flavored with coffee.

coffeehouse

a place that serves coffee drinks and other nonalcoholic drinks, as well as cakes, pastries, and other light foods. A coffeehouse is more of a social gathering place than a place for meals.

EATING & DRINKING

coffee shop
an inexpensive restaurant, with a counter and booths, that serves a wide range of food, from breakfast to sandwiches, salads, and simple dinner dishes. Many of these restaurants offer customers coffee as soon as they sit down, and often don't charge for refills. A coffee shop is also a place that sells European coffee beverages and other light refreshments.

cold cuts
cooked or preserved meats such as ham, turkey, roast beef, or pastrami, sliced thinly and eaten cold, especially in sandwiches and salads.

cold drink
another word for a **soft drink**, commonly used in the South.

coleslaw
a salad of grated cabbage, carrot, and onion mixed with mayonnaise.

concentrate
fruit juice with most of the water taken out of it that is sold in cans that are kept in a freezer. To make juice, you mix three cans of water with the concentrate.

cookie
a thin, sweet, crisp or chewy cake, often with nuts or chocolate added; *biscuit*.

cookie sheet
a flat metal tray for baking cookies, biscuits, etc.; *baking tray*.

cookout
an outdoor party where food is cooked over an open fire; a **barbecue.**

cornbread
slightly sweet cake made with cornmeal.

corn dog
a **frankfurter** covered in cornmeal batter and fried.

corned beef
beef that is preserved in salt and spices, and used as a filling for sandwiches; *salt beef*.

cornmeal
ground corn (*maize*) used like flour.

cracker

a thin, dry, crispy bread, often eaten with foods such as cheese, soup, and chili; *savory biscuit.*

crepe

a very thin pancake, usually rolled around a filling or covered in a sauce.

custard

a sweet dish of milk, eggs, and sugar that is baked until it is set. Americans do not pour liquid custard over their desserts.

a Danish, a Danish pastry

a sweet, buttery pastry, often filled with fruit and topped with icing, eaten at breakfast and with coffee.

decaf, decaffeinated

decaf coffee, tea, or soft drinks have had the caffeine taken out.

deli, delicatessen

a store, or a counter inside a larger store, that sells food that is ready to eat, especially items such as cheeses and cold cuts. They also prepare and serve fresh sandwiches to take out, and some delis have tables where you can eat.

dill pickles

cucumbers preserved in vinegar and salt, flavored with dill and garlic. Dill pickles can be whole, sliced into long wedges, or in thin round slices.

diner

an inexpensive restaurant, with a counter and booths, that serves simple, basic food.

doggy bag

a bag or box containing leftover food from a meal eaten at a restaurant. Doggy bags were originally used for taking food home as a treat for a pet, but they are now used to save food so it is not wasted.

doughnut

a small, rich, fried cake. American doughnuts are ring-shaped unless they are filled with jam, in which case they do not have a hole in the middle.

draft (beer)

beer that is drawn from a keg or cask.

dress
to prepare a sandwich with additional ingredients such as lettuce, tomatoes, pickles, and sauces.

egg roll
a Chinese food made of chopped meat or vegetables rolled in egg dough and deep fried; the term *spring roll* is also used.

egg salad
a dish made with hard-boiled eggs, celery, pickles, and mayonnaise; *egg mayonnaise*.

English muffin
a small, yeasty roll that is split and toasted, and eaten warm with butter and jam. Similar to what is known in the U.K. as a *muffin*.

entrée
the main course in a meal, especially one in a restaurant.

farmer's market
a market where farmers and food producers sell their produce directly to the public. They are known as a source of high quality and often organic food.

flapjack
another word for a **pancake.** The thick, sweet oat cakes known in Britain as flapjacks are not known in the United States, although **granola bars** are similar.

frank, frankfurter
a long, reddish sausage made of beef or pork, and more recently, turkey. Usually eaten in a bun; also called a **hot dog.**

French dressing
a salad dressing that is both sweet and sour, slightly creamy, and usually bright orange in color. Although some cookbooks refer to the mix of oil, vinegar, and seasonings as French dressing, the term usually refers to the bottled orange stuff. "Vinaigrette" is used to refer to oil and vinegar dressing.

fries, French fries
long thin pieces of fried potato; *chips*.

frosting
the thick, sweet, creamy substance used to cover and decorate cakes; *icing* is also used.

fusion cuisine
a style of cooking that takes elements from various cuisines, especially Asian, and mixes them with more traditional styles and ingredients.

go Dutch
If a couple or a group of people go Dutch, they each pay for their share of the bill.

graham cracker
a sweet, rectangular cracker made from whole-wheat flour. Often used crushed for making pie crusts. This is the closest thing in the United States to a *digestive biscuit*.

granola
a breakfast food made of oats and dried fruit or nuts. Granola is mixed with honey or maple syrup and baked, so it is crunchy, unlike muesli. It is eaten cold with milk.

granola bar
a snack bar made of sweetened rolled oats and dried fruit or nuts.

griddle
a flat, heavy pan for cooking things such as pancakes.

grill
a metal rack placed over an open fire, as on a barbecue, for cooking food.

grilled cheese sandwich
a hot fried sandwich typically made of melted American cheese on white bread. Despite the name, it is not made on a grill, but in a frying pan or on a griddle.

grits
ground white corn or hominy boiled and served as a side dish, often as part of breakfast. Grits are eaten especially in the South.

ground beef
a piece of meat that is ground up for use in hamburgers, meatloaf, and chili. Also known as **hamburger;** mince.

gyoza
small pockets of dough that are filled with meat or vegetables and fried or steamed; a Japanese dish.

EATING & DRINKING

gyro
a sandwich made with sliced, roasted lamb, onions, and toma-toes in pita bread. This is the closest thing to a kebab in the United States, unless you go to a Mediterranean restaurant.

half-and-half
a mixture of equal parts milk and cream, used in coffee and sometimes eaten with cereal.

hamburger
another word for **ground beef.**

hash browns
shredded and fried potatoes, usually served at breakfast.

hero
another word for a **submarine sandwich.**

hibachi
a small, portable charcoal-burning barbecue grill.

hoagie
another name for a **submarine sandwich.**

hotcake
another word for a **pancake.**

hot dog
a cooked **frankfurter** served in a long, soft bun, with condi-ments such as mustard, ketchup, onions, and relish.

Italian dressing
a salad dressing made of oil, vinegar, and seasonings. It can also include Parmesan or Romano cheese, and is also available in a "creamy" version.

jelly
a soft, thick, sweet food made from fruit juice. Jelly is like jam without the pieces of fruit in it. It is used as a spread on toast or an ingredient in peanut butter and jelly sandwiches.

keg
a large barrel for beer, usually found in bars. Kegs can also be bought from liquor stores for consumption at large parties.

kegger
a big party, usually organized by college students, where beer from kegs is served.

knish
baked or fried dough filled with potatoes, meat, or cheese.

Kool-Aid™
an artificially fruit-flavored powder used for making a sweet drink.

layer cake
a frosted cake made of layers of sponge cake that have filling between them.

lemonade
a drink made with water, sugar, and fresh lemon juice. Nowadays it is often made from a flavored powder mix or frozen concentrate. The soft drink known in the rest of the world as "lemonade" is usually referred to by its brand name or is called "lemon-lime soda."

link
a small long round piece of sausage, fried and served at breakfast.

liquor
"hard" alcohol such as vodka, whiskey, and gin, as opposed to beer or wine.

longneck
a beer bottle with a long neck.

lowfat milk
milk with only a small amount of milk fat in it, usually one to two percent; *semi-skimmed milk.*

maitre d'(hotel)
the headwaiter in a restaurant, especially an expensive one.

meatloaf
a dish typical of American home cooking, made from ground beef, spices, and tomato sauce, formed into a loaf and then cooked in the oven.

microbrewery
a small brewery that brews its own beer to sell at the brewery or within a small region.

mimosa
a cocktail made from champagne and orange juice; *buck's fizz.*

EATING & DRINKING

mixer
an electric device with metal parts for beating or mixing ingredients; *electric whisk*.

Monterey Jack
a bland yellow to white cheese often used as an ingredient in Mexican food.

muffin
a sweet baked breakfast bread that is a lot like a small cake.

nonfat milk
milk with less than 0.5 percent milk fat; *skimmed milk*.

nuke
a slang term meaning to cook or heat up food in a microwave oven.

on the side
Food that is served on the side is not mixed in with the other food on your plate. Hamburgers usually come with fries on the side, and if you do not want much dressing on your salad, you can ask for it on the side.

over easy
eggs that are fried on both sides, with the yolk still slightly runny.

pancake
a type of thin cake cooked in a pan or on a griddle on the stovetop. Eaten at breakfast topped with butter and syrup or fruit. Americans do not eat pancakes with lime and icing sugar.

pancake turner
another word for a **spatula**.

patty
a thin, round piece of chopped meat, usually hamburger or sausage.

pickle
a cucumber, either whole or in slices, that is preserved in vinegar.

poorboy, poboy
another word for a **submarine sandwich**, used mostly in Louisiana.

pop
another word for a **soft drink**, used mainly in the Midwest and West.

powdered sugar
fine white sugar; *icing sugar*.

prix fixe menu
a menu that includes a set of choices for each course of a meal and costs a fixed price; *set menu*.

pudding
a soft, sweet, cooked dessert made from milk and a thickener such as flour or cornstarch, eaten cold. Popular flavors are vanilla, chocolate, and butterscotch. Americans don't often eat traditional baked and steamed puddings. Dessert is never called "pudding."

pumpernickel
a type of dark rye bread with a slightly sour taste.

ranch dressing
a creamy salad dressing made with sour cream and/or buttermilk and seasonings.

regular
used to refer to the medium size of a food or drink order: "I'll have a regular coke and fries with that, please." Regular can also be used to say that something comes in its original or plain state, so "a regular Coke" may also mean an original Coke, rather than a diet or decaf version.

relish
chopped, sweet pickles used on hot dogs and sandwiches.

Reuben sandwich
a hot sandwich made with rye bread and filled with corned beef, Swiss cheese, and sauerkraut.

rye bread
a type of bread made with rye flour, which has a slightly sour taste and is often flavored with caraway seeds. It is used especially for making sandwiches.

salad
a mixture of vegetables such as lettuce, tomatoes, cucumbers, etc., covered with a dressing, and served as a side dish or a main dish.

EATING & DRINKING

It is never used to mean "lettuce," and it is not an ingredient in a sandwich, unless it is something like chicken or egg salad.

salsa
a Mexican relish made from tomatoes, onions, and chilies; usually served with corn chips for dipping. The term is also used for any number of similar relishes.

saltine
a thin cracker that is sprinkled with salt. Saltines are lighter than *cream crackers*, but the taste is similar.

sausage
chopped and seasoned meat, usually pork. Americans usually use the word as an uncountable noun. It is often eaten for breakfast in **links** or **patties.** Sausages are not known as *bangers.*

sauté
to fry food quickly in a shallow pan.

schnitzel
a slice of meat, usually veal, that is broiled or fried.

screwdriver
a cocktail made from vodka and orange juice.

server
someone who serves food and drinks to people in a restaurant.

sharp
used to describe the flavor of cheese when it is very strong; *mature.*

sherbet
a frozen dessert flavored with fruit juice and also containing water, sugar, and milk or egg white.

side (order)
a portion of something such as vegetables that is ordered in addition to a main dish: "Can I have a side of coleslaw with the ribs, please?"

side salad
a small salad that is served before or along with a main dish.

sift
to put flour or sugar through a sieve to remove any large particles; *sieve.*

skillet
a frying pan.

skim milk
milk with less than 0.5 percent milk fat; *skimmed milk.*

soda
another word for a **soft drink**, used in the Northeast. The original word was "soda pop," and different parts of the country shortened it to "soda" or "pop."

soft-boiled egg
an egg that is boiled in the shell for a short time and is usually eaten in an egg cup; *boiled egg.*

soft drink
a drink without alcohol in it, that has bubbles and is sold in cans or bottles.

sommelier
someone who helps you choose wine in a restaurant; *wine steward.*

sourdough bread
a type of white bread made with a fermented dough that gives it a sour taste, originally from northern California.

Southwestern cuisine
a type of cooking that uses ingredients that are typical of the states that border Mexico.

spatula
a kitchen tool with a broad, flat blade that is used for turning cooking food; *fish slice.* A rubber spatula has a flexible rubber blade that is used for mixing and spreading.

strainer
a kitchen tool like a metal net with a handle; *sieve.*

stuffing
a mixture of bread pieces, meat broth, and spices used to fill turkeys and chickens when they are roasted.

submarine, sub
a sandwich made on a long loaf of soft, white bread and containing one or more types of meat, cheese, lettuce, tomatoes, pickles, and condiments.

EATING & DRINKING

sunnyside up
Eggs that are sunnyside up are fried on only one side.

sweet pickles
cucumbers preserved in vinegar, sugar, and spices.

sweets
the word "sweets" refers to any sweet food such as cakes, cookies, and ice cream, not just the chocolates and sugary foods eaten especially by children (➪ **candy**). "Sweet" is not used to refer to dessert.

syrup
a thick sweet sauce eaten on pancakes. In the United States, this is nearly always maple syrup, unless it is made from a particular fruit, blueberry being the most common. Real maple syrup comes from the sweet sap of the sugar maple tree, although most syrup is actually artificially "maple-flavored."

takeout
food from a restaurant that is taken away to be eaten somewhere else. Usually used as an adjective rather than a noun: "We had some takeout Chinese last night."

tavern
a place that serves only beer and wine rather than stronger alcohol, and that may serve food.

to go
used to say that food will not be eaten at the restaurant where it was bought: "I'll have a turkey sandwich, and make that to go."

tortilla
a flat Mexican bread made of cornmeal (a corn tortilla) or wheat flour (a flour tortilla).

weenie
an informal word for a **wiener**.

wiener
another word for a **frankfurter**.

wrap
a flour tortilla wrapped around a variety of fillings.

zap
a slang term meaning to cook or heat up food in a microwave oven.

Chapter Four
Getting Around

🔑 Key Confusables:

British	American
aeroplane	= *airplane*
car park	= *parking lot*
coach	= *bus*
driving licence	= *driver's license*
gearbox	= *transmission*
give way	= *yield*
lorry	= *truck*
motorway	= *highway, freeway, interstate*
number plate	= *license plate*
pavement, footpath	= *sidewalk*
petrol	= *gasoline, gas*
railway	= *railroad*
return ticket	= *round trip ticket*
road	= *street*
roundabout	= *traffic circle, rotary*
single	= *one-way ticket*
transport	= *transportation*
turnoff	= *exit, off-ramp*
underground, tube	= *subway*

🔑 Key Americanism:

Americans often use *automobile* or *auto* when talking about cars, especially as an adjective, as in *automobile industry* or *auto insurance*. They do not *motor* or drive *motorcars*.

🔑 Key Grammar:

The word *street* is used more than *road* by Americans. *Roads* are usually out in rural areas, not in towns. Americans do not use the definite article when they use the name of a highway or road, such as "the M-25."

Americans say:
The café is three blocks away.
We took I-90 to Montana.
The hotel is on Geary Street.
I'd like to rent a car.

Americans *do not* say:
The café is three streets away.
We took the I-90 to Montana.
The hotel is in Geary Street.
I'd like to hire a car.

⚷ Key Cultural Points:

Gasoline is cheap, cars are affordable, and distances are great, so cars are the most logical form of transportation in the United States. Most people own a car, and except in large cities, public transportation hardly exists at all. The sight of someone walking any long distance in a town or suburban area is fairly strange. Americans will drive from one side of a shopping mall to the other rather than walk the whole way and back.

When going between cities, flying is the fastest means of transportation.

> **!** **Warning:** Americans drive on the right side of the road.

. . . .

Cars, Cars, Cars

There could hardly be a more car-crazy country than the United States. Driving is the most popular means of transportation—walking isn't really considered an option when it comes to getting around, and since buildings and shopping areas are so spread out, a car really is the most logical choice.

Most cities in the United States do not have much in the way of public transportation, with the exception of larger places like New York, Chicago, Boston, and San Francisco. Most cities and towns are designed with cars rather than pedestrians in mind. In fact, many U.S. cities are almost impossible to get around in without a car, and people rarely walk any farther than from their doors to their cars and back again.

Generally speaking, American cities are flat and square, with San Francisco being a notable exception. There, city planners took the basic grid design that was used when laying out most cities and just laid it on the area's many steep hills rather than building around them. In general, though, it is pretty hard to get lost in an American town because of this grid. Streets and avenues cross each other and form **blocks.** This is the basic unit into which cities are broken down, and people use blocks when giving directions or talking about a specific place. For example someone might say, "She lives a couple of blocks from here."

Americans are likely to give directions by talking about blocks rather than streets: "Turn left and go up three blocks."

Traffic Signals

GETTING AROUND

The United States has some traffic signals that are used in other countries. On smaller streets, most **intersections** (cross streets) have a big, red, octagonal **stop sign.** Drivers must come to a complete stop and make sure that there is no oncoming traffic before going on.

Another frequently used traffic signal is the **yield** sign—a white triangle with a red border and the word YIELD on it. This sign appears on ramps leading onto highways or major streets. Drivers should slow down or stop, and let traffic on the busier street go by.

Roundabouts, known as **traffic circles** or **rotaries,** are not used very much in the United States Instead, there are **four-**

way intersections where two streets meet. The car arriving at the intersection first goes first, and after that the next car to its right. There are occasional **three-way intersections,** too. These intersections are marked by red stop signs with "4-WAY" or "3-WAY" underneath them.

Generally though, traffic lights (also called **stoplights**) are used a lot more often at intersections, and *only* at intersections, rather than in the middle of a block. The lights are usually suspended above the street, although they can also be on the corner to the right of the intersection. Many traffic lights also display an arrow signal for turning left. In some states, drivers can make a right turn on a red light, provided there is no traffic coming toward them in the first lane.

Most streets run in both directions, but in many downtown areas a system of one-way streets is used. A white arrow sign with a black border will tell you which direction you can go.

Streets that are not through streets are called **dead-end streets** and have yellow signs at their entrances.

Yellow lines are used to divide the street if traffic moves in opposite directions. Larger streets are divided by a **median** or **median strip,** a paved or sometimes landscaped area in the middle of the street. There is a variety of regional names for the median—"mall" in upstate New York, "meridian" or "boulevard"

in parts of the Midwest, and "neutral ground" in Louisiana. (This latter term dates back to the time when the state was populated by rival French and Spanish factions. The French stayed on one side of the roads and the Spanish on the other, leaving a neutral area in the middle.)

People new to driving in the United States should be aware that a lane to the far right or left may suddenly and without much warning become a **turning lane** *or an* **exit lane***. Once in it, drivers must follow the direction indicated on it.*

Jammin'

All these cars on the American roads have made for terrible traffic and pollution problems. The words **gridlock** (on city streets) and **traffic jam** (on streets or highways) are commonly used when talking about traffic that does not move. Some cities have tried to ease the problem by setting up **car pool** or **high occupancy vehicle** lanes that can be used only by cars with more than one passenger.

All new cars sold in the U.S. run on unleaded gasoline only, and cars have to pass **smog tests** or **emissions tests.** The requirements for the smog tests vary from state to state. There are no tests for a car's general roadworthiness, which is obvious if you look around at some of the rusty old vehicles that people drive until they fall apart.

"Tailback" is not used in American English. A tailback is a position on a football team. Use **backup** *instead.*

On the Road

In many large and mid-sized cities, the grid system has been broken up by the arrival of **freeways** and **interstate highways.** Freeways are high-speed roads that cross entire cities. In major cities, they can be enormous, with up to eight lanes and several levels, especially where several of these roads meet. Although traffic can be horrendous on freeways, especially during **rush hour,** they are generally a fast and efficient way of getting through a city, as there is no stopping on them and traffic flows in and out of them more or less smoothly.

Other names for large highways are **thruway, expressway,** and **turnpike.** You sometimes have to pay to use these: you take a ticket from a tollbooth, and when you leave it, you pay a small fee. The freeway got its name from the fact that you don't have to pay to use it.

Interstate

Freeways are sometimes part of an interstate highway. The interstate highway system is a network of highways paid for by the federal government that connect the whole of the country. Interstates have the initial *I* followed by a number indicating the route, such as *I-90.*

Older United States highways that existed before the freeways were built have U.S. in front of the number, such as *U.S. 99,* but most people use just the number. U.S. highways that go through towns often have stoplights on them, whereas interstates do not.

U.S. Highway

State routes are roads within a particular state. They usually have the initials *SR* in front of the number, and they vary tremendously in size and quality. The symbol for each of these routes is different in every state.

State Route

North–south routes are marked with odd numbers, while even numbers mean that a road runs east–west.

Some interstate highways span thousands of miles, such as I-10, which runs from Los Angeles, California, to Jacksonville, Florida. While they often run through larger cities, interstates don't usually go through small towns. These tend to be located off to one side of the interstate.

Interstate highways were designed with drivers' safety and comfort in mind, so they tend to be wide and straight, making for somewhat monotonous driving. It is probably because of this, and the fact that Americans will drive hundreds of miles at a stretch, that **cruise control** comes as standard equipment in many new cars.

Places to Stop

Driving is probably the best way to get a real sense of just how big the country is. When you're on the road, it's not uncommon to drive for hundreds of miles without seeing many other cars, let alone any towns. Between towns, there are **rest areas** about every fifty miles, marked by blue signs. They offer little besides a place to stop for a rest, toilets, and sometimes vending machines. Some, but not all, have picnic tables.

Another option is the **truck stop**, a diner or restaurant that caters mainly to drivers of large trucks called **tractor-trailer rigs** or **semis,** but that sometimes also serves the general public. Otherwise, it is quite easy to pull off into a small town for gas and refreshments. Blue signs on the road clearly indicate what kinds of facilities are available in an upcoming town. And of course it's hard to miss those golden arches shining like beacons above almost every town.

Speed Limits

People used to driving in Europe may find that Americans drive incredibly slowly, even on what are supposed to be high-speed highways. This goes back to 1974, when the national speed limit on U.S. highways was set at 55 miles per hour (mph) at the height of the energy crisis. As of 1987, the limit was raised to 65 miles per hour on rural interstate highways. In 1995, states were given authority by the federal government to set the highway speed limits within their own states. This means that the speed limit can change unexpectedly when crossing state lines. So while the speed limit in, say, Texas may be 70, it can drop to 65 as soon as a car goes into New Mexico.

State highways and county roads usually have lower speed limits than interstate highways. Within cities and towns, speed limits are again lower, ranging from about 45 mph on major streets to 20 mph in school zones. If an interstate goes through a city, a high speed is maintained on it, but **on-ramps** and **off-ramps** have lower limits, especially if they have sharp curves. High-speed roads also have a minimum speed, usually 15 to 20 mph less than the maximum speed allowed. In addition, some speed limits drop 5 to 10 mph at night.

100 kilometers per hour is about 60 miles per hour. If you rent a car in the United States, the miles per hour will be the bigger numbers on the **speedometer**.

Speed limits and other traffic regulations are enforced by a combination of state, county, and city police. Interstates and other federal highways are patrolled by **state troopers** or the **highway patrol**, often on motorcycles. State troopers usually operate outside of cities and towns. State highways are usually patrolled by the county sheriff's officers, while city police officers deal with traffic within cities and towns.

> **!** **Warning:** *If you are pulled over,* **do not get out of your car.** *Wait until the officer comes up to your window, and be very, very polite. You will be asked for your driver's license, vehicle registration, and proof of insurance, so get it all ready for the officer to inspect. Do not argue with an officer if you get a ticket. If you think you did nothing wrong, and you really think it's worth it to argue the point in traffic court, follow the directions on the ticket, which tell you what to do.*

Driver's Licenses

All drivers must have a **driver's license** from the state in which they live. Licenses are issued by each state's **Department of Motor Vehicles (DMV),** and in some cases by the county clerk's office. The minimum age for obtaining a regular driver's license is usually sixteen, but again this varies from state to state. Teenagers under the age of eighteen can get a license if their parents officially agree, and they are usually required to take a full driver's education course as well. Such courses are often taught in high schools, as an after-school activity.

All drivers must pass a state's written test, covering knowledge of traffic and safety regulations, as well as a practical driving test on the road. Licenses always have the driver's picture on them, along with information such as physical characteristics, age, Social Security number, and address.

Most Americans always carry their licenses because it is their main form of identification, and is used for a number of things such as cashing checks, opening bank accounts, and proving a person's age when buying alcohol or entering a bar. The DMV can also issue identification cards to nondrivers that look just like driver's licenses but clearly show that the person is not allowed to drive. Licenses have to be renewed periodically, every four to six years.

Many states operate a penalty points system for traffic offenses. Drivers who accumulate a certain number of points in a year may have their licenses suspended, which is a fate worse than death to the car-dependent American.

Insurance and Registration

Auto insurance is required in most states. Although requirements vary from state to state, drivers are usually covered by **liability insurance** and **personal injury protection** insurance. Drivers must have proof of insurance with them in the car at all times.

The other document that must be carried is the car's **Certificate of Title** or **Certificate of Ownership.** This includes the owner's name and address, as well as the car's license plate number. A new certificate is necessary every time the vehicle is sold.

Public Transportation

At the beginning of the twentieth century, **public transportation** or **mass transit** systems were very much a part of American life. However, the structure of American cities started changing in the years after World War II. The growth of suburbs and the spread of business development to country areas combined with increased car ownership to mean the death of most existing public transportation. It didn't help that the major oil companies helped pay to tear up the railroads and build highways.

Now, all that remains in most American cities is a relatively limited bus service. Large, densely populated cities such as New York, Boston, Washington, Atlanta, San Francisco, and Chicago are the exception. These cities have networks of buses and rail rapid transit (**subways** and **elevated trains**), as well as commuter railroad connections serving extended metropolitan areas.

*In American English, **subway** always refers to a network of rapid transit trains that run underground.*

Underpass *is the word used for a road that runs under another road, but they are usually for cars to drive on, rather than for pedestrians. The word **exit** is used to show the way out of a station or other public place, rather than the more literal "Way Out," which Americans think is funny when they encounter it in Britain. It sounds too much like 1960s hippie slang.*

In other cities, public transportation consists primarily of buses, which often operate only on limited routes or on an infrequent **schedule. Streetcars** are still in operation in some cities such as San Francisco, New Orleans, and Philadelphia, although they tend to be more of a tourist attraction than a reliable form of public transportation.

Streetcars are also known as **cable cars** *and* **trolleys**, *but "tram" is not commonly used.*

Taxis

Taxis, or **cabs,** do travel the streets in downtown areas of large cities looking for customers, but you will notice that in most cities there are far fewer taxis than you would expect. Many towns and cities only have **on-call** service for taxis: you must call ahead and order a taxi rather than trying to find one on the street.

Car services usually provide very nice cars but charge more than taxis do; the advantage of a car service is that your fare is fixed ahead of time, so that you know the cost of your ride before you get in. Be sure to ask what the fare will be when you order the car. Taxi fares are based on meters, so if you are in heavy traffic, the cost of a cab ride can rise very quickly.

Train Travel

The United States has one of the largest **railroad** networks in the world, yet it is used mostly for freight. The number of passengers carried on those railroads is very low. Because distances are so great, air travel has replaced train travel for most people. After all, why travel for three days when you can fly across the country in about six hours?

However, trains provide a comfortable and leisurely way to see the country for passengers who have a lot of time or hate flying. Long-distance railroads are operated by Amtrak, a company formed in the early 1970s to take over and run all the dying railroad companies around the country. The cheapest tickets on trains are known as **coach.** Tickets for all types of transportation are known as **one way**, for single tickets, and **round trip**, for return tickets.

Train tickets should be bought before traveling; on longer trips, you can't get on the train at all without a ticket, and on commuter trips, you usually have to pay a higher fare if you buy the ticket from the **conductor** on board the train. (The person who drives the train is an **engineer.**) Arriving and departing trains are announced by **track** number, rather than by platform number, although the area passengers stand on while waiting for a train is still referred to as the platform. The compartments on a train that passengers travel in are known as **cars** or **coaches;** for long trips, you can book a berth in a **sleeper.**

Long-Distance Buses

The bus is the cheapest form of long-distance transportation in the United States, and the one with the most extensive system of routes, taking people from the largest of cities to all but the smallest and remotest towns in the country. You'll meet a lot of interesting people on bus trips, but be prepared to share your life story. Trips tends to be long, and people talk a lot.

Long-distance buses are not called "coaches" in American English.

The largest American bus operator is Greyhound Lines, which serves all major cities and towns. Travel to smaller towns is usually provided by local and regional bus companies.

Bicycling

Americans do ride bikes, but mostly for exercise or for fun. Getting around a city on a bike can be dangerous, because most cities do not have special bike lanes. If they do, they often end suddenly when a street gets too narrow for that extra lane. Bicyclists who ride on streets are expected to follow all the traffic laws, and you are not supposed to ride a bike on a sidewalk, but many people ignore these rules.

Air Travel

There are so many airlines, national and regional, that flying is an economical and popular form of transportation for many Americans, and it's really the best way of covering long distances in the United States. Businesspeople fly all over the country, and it's not uncommon to "commute" between cities by plane. **Frequent flyer** programs that offer rewards to passengers who rack up a lot of travel miles are very popular, and you can earn air miles by using special credit cards or even by using particular phone companies.

Some airlines operate on a **no-frills** basis, offering rock-bottom fares, but slightly less comfortable planes and little more than peanuts and pretzels to eat. Most airlines serve free soft drinks, but all alcoholic beverages in coach class must be paid for in cash.

Airlines regularly **overbook** domestic flights, so it is important to check in on time to avoid being being **bumped** off a flight. However, airlines do offer compensation in the form of cash or free flights to passengers who volunteer to give up their seats on overbooked flights.

When it comes to international flights, prices to and from the United States are extremely competitive. **Consolidators,** or agencies that sell international airline tickets at massive discounts, offer the cheapest flights.

Something that might come as a surprise to people used to traveling internationally is that American duty free is nowhere near as developed a concept as it is in, say, Europe. Many smaller international airports have little more than a cart selling a few varieties of whiskey, cigarettes, and some perfume. Larger airports have larger stores, but they tend to specialize in alcohol, cigarettes, and cosmetics. Duty-free goods must be purchased in the airport shop, but they are not handed over to the passengers. Instead, they are delivered to them when they are actually boarding the plane.

Americans usually refer to luggage as **baggage**, *and the place where you buy your tickets is a* **ticket counter**.

Getting Out of the Airport

Buses and taxis are the usual means of getting into a city from an airport, unless someone is picking you up. Outside the **bag-**

gage claim (where you pick up your bags), there are signs that tell you where to stand to wait for a bus or a taxi. Buses are the cheapest, but be sure that you know where the bus is going. There is usually a transportation information desk near the baggage claim. Airport buses usually have stops at major hotels, but they do not make request stops.

Bus drivers do not usually give change, so ask what the exact fare is.

Taxis sometimes have fixed fares to city centers, so be sure to ask before you get in. In New York, for instance, there is a $35 fixed fare, but some taxi drivers do not post this and will charge whatever the meter reads—up to $80 in heavy traffic—for the same trip.

Shuttles are a cheaper way to go if you are not in a hurry. These are vans that carry about ten people, and they do not leave the airport until the van is full. They will take you directly to the address you want, but you may be the last person to be dropped off, so be aware that the trip may take some time.

> ❗ **Warning:** *There may be unmarked cars with drivers who slowly drive by and call out to people who are standing in lines for buses, taxis, and shuttles, offering fixed-fare rides into town. These people are not licensed to carry passengers, and you should not accept a ride from them.*

Left Luggage

Americans don't use the term "left luggage." They would probably guess that you meant the **lost and found**—the lost property office. There are no guarded rooms where you can leave your bags for a short time in American train stations and airports. There are, however, coin-operated lockers of different sizes.

If you need to leave your luggage for a short time at a hotel, you go to the **bell station**.

Hotels

Hotels in the United States are similar to those around the world. There are, however, a few differences to be aware of.

The word "concierge" is used only in large, expensive hotels; the usual term for the place that you check in is the **front desk.** A **bellhop** is the person who will carry your bags to your room for you, and the **bell station** is where you can ask the **bell captain** to call a taxi for you, and where you can leave your luggage if it is too early to check in, or if you have checked out but still need to store your bags for a short time.

American hotels usually have separate smoking and non-smoking rooms, so tell the desk clerk if you have a preference when you check in. Some hotels are smoke-free, so be sure to ask before you book a room.

Rooms are called **singles** (with one bed), **doubles** (with two beds), and **suites** (with more than one room). Any bed is usually a double bed—big enough for two people to sleep in—and families of four often rent just one double room. You can often get a camp bed for an extra person—called a **cot**—put in a room for a small extra charge.

Private bathrooms are nearly always in the rooms, unless it is a very cheap hotel. This is not called an "en-suite" bathroom; the idea that one would not have a bathroom in the room is so foreign to Americans that there is not a special term for this. You don't have to ask "is there a private bathroom in the room?"

Motels

Motels are a uniquely American invention. The word means "motor hotel," and this type of hotel became popular as the highway network replaced rail travel.

Motels are generally cheaper than hotels, and the rooms are usually entered from outdoors or a covered balcony rather than from an indoor hall. You drive up to the motel office to check in, then drive to a parking place next to your room. You can see from the road whether there are free rooms in the motel: a VACANCY sign means there are rooms, and NO VACANCY means the motel is full. Motels do not have meal service, although there may be restaurants nearby.

Bed-and-Breakfasts

A bed-and-breakfast, or B&B, in the United States is not a cheap and possibly dirty alternative to a hotel room. B&Bs are usually in beautiful older homes that have been lovingly decorated, and the breakfasts are freshly made and large. Along with the usual eggs, bacon, sausage, and toast, you will probably have a choice of freshly baked goods such as muffins and biscuits, and home-made granola and other cereals. The juice and coffee are always fresh.

B&Bs are usually in country areas and smaller towns, although there are some in cities. You do often have to share a bathroom with other guests in a B&B.

. . . .

Glossary of American Terms

3-way intersection
a place where one street meets another but does not cross it; *T-junction*. Drivers must come to a complete stop, and the first car to have reached the intersection proceeds first. Priority then goes to the next car on the right.

4-way intersection
a place where two streets cross. Drivers must come to a complete stop, and the first car to have reached the intersection proceeds first. Priority then goes to the next car on the right.

bell captain
the main person in charge of the bellhops in a hotel.

bellhop
someone who takes your luggage to your room in a hotel.

bell station
a small desk in the lobby of a hotel where the bell captain will arrange to have a bellhop take your luggage or to have a taxi collect you, and will also store your luggage for short periods.

billboard
a large sign on the side of a road or on a building, used for advertising; *hoarding*.

block
the rectangular areas formed by streets as they cross each other, or the space between one street and the next.

bump
to put passengers who check in late on the next available flight to their destination.

cab
another word for a **taxi**.

cable car
a vehicle for public transportation that is pulled along by an underground cable on a fixed route through a city.

car
one of the wagons that link up to form a train.

carpool
to share a ride with people who work together or go to school together. Also used as a noun (car pool).

car service
a privately owned company that provides car transportation if you call ahead of time. Fares for car services are fixed.

Certificate of Title/Ownership
an official document that proves that a particular vehicle belongs to a particular person.

coach
economy class on airplanes and trains; also, a compartment for passengers on a train.

conductor
someone who checks and sells tickets on a train.

consolidator
an agency that sells international airline tickets at reduced

prices. They work by buying up blocks of tickets and then selling them at a discount; *bucket shop.*

cot

a small, fold-out bed for one person; *camp bed.*

crosswalk

a specially marked part of a street where people can cross; *zebra crossing.*

cruise control

a device in a car that holds it at a particular speed, so that the driver does not have to keep their foot on the gas pedal. This is particularly useful when driving on long, straight roads.

dead battery

a car battery that doesn't work; *flat battery.*

Department of Motor Vehicles (DMV)

the part of a state's government that deals with the registration of automobiles and that issues driver's licenses.

detour

an alternative route to be followed by cars when there is an accident or work is being done on a street or road; *diversion.*

doorman

someone who welcomes you to a hotel, helps you take your luggage inside, and calls taxis for you.

downtown

the central part of a city, where many businesses are found.

driver's license

an official document showing that a person is allowed to drive a car.

eighteen-wheeler

an informal term for a **tractor-trailer rig.**

elevated trains

a network of rapid transit trains that are raised above street level. In Chicago it is known as "the el."

emergency brake

a separate braking device in a car used when parking or if the regular brakes fail; *hand brake.*

emissions test
another word for a **smog test.**

engineer
someone who drives a train.

exit
a road for leaving a highway or freeway; also called an **off-ramp**; *slip road.* An exit is also a door you can use to leave a building; *way out.*

exit lane
a lane on a highway or freeway that leads to an exit. Drivers must exit once they are in this lane.

expressway
a major high-speed road with many lanes.

flat, flat tire
a tire that has lost some of the air inside it; *puncture.*

freeway
a major high-speed road with many lanes.

freight train
a train used for carrying goods around the country; *goods train.*

frequent flyer
someone who flies a lot, especially on business. It is also the program run by an airline that gives frequent passengers free flights, upgrades, and other bonuses when they accumulate a certain number of flying miles.

front desk
the place where you check in at a hotel; *concierge desk.*

gas pedal
the pedal in a car that gives it fuel in order to make it move; *accelerator.*

grade crossing
a place where a road or street crosses a railroad line; *level crossing.*

gridlock
bad traffic congestion; the name comes from the fact that most American cities are laid out in a grid pattern.

high occupancy vehicle (HOV)

a car with more than just one person in it. HOVs are given priority in some cities in an attempt to cut down on traffic.

highway

a major road that goes between cities or towns.

highway patrol

the state police agency that is in charge of patrolling interstates and other highways within a state.

hood

the hinged metal piece that covers a car's engine; *bonnet*.

interstate

a major road that goes from one state to another.

jaywalking

the illegal act of crossing a street in a careless way, or not at a crosswalk.

liability insurance

auto insurance that covers drivers if they hurt another person or their property.

license plate

the metal sign placed at the front and back of a car showing the letters and numbers that identify it and what state it is from; *number plate*.

median (strip)

the narrow, paved area in the middle of a major street or highway that divides traffic traveling in opposite directions.

merge

to join the flow of traffic on a highway or freeway without stopping or slowing down.

muffler

a piece of equipment on a car that helps to reduce the noise made by the engine; *silencer*.

no-frills airline

airlines that provide a very basic service in exchange for very low airfares.

off-ramp
a road for leaving a highway or freeway; also called an **exit**; *slip road*.

on-call
used to talk about a taxi service that is available only if you call ahead to order a ride.

one-way ticket
a ticket to go somewhere but not return; *single ticket*.

on-ramp
a road for entering a highway or freeway; *slip road*.

overbook
to sell too many tickets for a particular scheduled flight.

overpass
an elevated road that goes over another road; *flyover*.

pass
to go faster than another car on a highway in order to get past it; *overtake*.

personal injury protection
a type of auto insurance that provides financial coverage for any personal injuries from an accident.

rest area
an area by the side of a road where drivers can pull off and rest, use the restroom, and buy drinks and snacks from vending machines; *lay-by*.

rotary
an intersection or junction with a circle in the middle around which traffic moves in one direction; *roundabout*.

round-trip ticket
a ticket to go somewhere and return; *return ticket*.

rush hour
the times of day when most people are on their way to and from work and school, usually between about 7:00 and 9:30 in the morning, and 4:30 and 7:00 at night.

schedule
a list of the times that a bus, train, ferry, etc. runs; *timetable*.

sedan

a car with four doors; *saloon*.

semitrailer, semi

a trailer with several sets of wheels designed to be pulled by a tractor, forming a **tractor-trailer rig**. A semi is also a truck with a cab and one long trailer attached to it; *semi-articulated lorry*.

shuttle

an airline that provides service between two major airports that are relatively close to each other, such as New York and Washington. It is also a vehicle or train that goes directly back and forth between two points, especially at an airport.

side mirror

the small, adjustable mirror at the side of a car; *wing mirror*.

smog test

a test to prove that your car is not producing unacceptable levels of pollution; *MOT*. The levels allowed vary from state to state. Some states require the test every year, and some every two to three years.

speedometer

the gauge that tells you how fast a car is going.

sport utility vehicle (SUV)

an off-road vehicle like a small, enclosed truck, now often driven by people in cities who don't ever need one.

standard

a car with a manual transmission; also called a **stick shift.**

state trooper

a member of the state police whose job is to patrol federal highways and interstates outside of cities and towns.

station wagon

a large car with extra space at the back rather than a trunk, popular with families; *estate car*.

stick shift

a car with a manual transmission: "Roy drives a stick shift." It is also the actual lever used for changing gears.

stoplight

a traffic light.

GETTING AROUND

stop sign
a large, red, octagonal traffic sign that indicates that drivers must come to a complete stop.

streetcar
a vehicle used for public transportation that moves along rails on a fixed route through a city.

subway
a network of rapid transit trains that run underground.

thruway
a major high-speed road with many lanes.

tire
the American spelling of *tyre*.

tractor-trailer rig
a large trailer with several sets of wheels pulled by a tractor truck, used for transporting goods; *articulated lorry*.

traffic circle
an intersection or junction with a circle in the middle around which traffic moves in one direction; *roundabout*.

transfer
a type of bus or train ticket that allows passengers to change to a different bus or train in order to reach their destination without paying for another ticket.

trolley
an electric vehicle used for public transportation that connects to overhead cables along fixed routes. It is also another word for **streetcar**.

truck stop
a roadside establishment mainly for drivers of tractor-trailer rigs, which sells fuel for the rigs and has a restaurant and rest area for drivers.

trunk
the enclosed space at the back of a car for carrying baggage, groceries, etc.; *boot*.

tune-up
a service in which a mechanic checks a car's engine to make sure that it runs well.

turning lane
a lane on a street or highway for turning. Drivers must turn if they are in a turning lane.

turnpike
a major highway on which drivers often have to pay a toll. They are usually found in the Northeast of the United States.

underpass
a road that goes under another road.

uptown
the outer or northern parts of a city, typically more residential and affluent in character than downtown areas.

van
a vehicle that can carry up to ten passengers or a lot of baggage. Vans in the United States do not usually have a cab (area for the driver in the front) that is separate from the main part of the vehicle. Vans are popular with families because they can fit the children, the dog, and all their gear into one vehicle. Vans are also used as airport **shuttles.**

vanity plate
a license plate that shows special letters or numbers that have been chosen by the owner of the car.

weigh station
a place at the side of a highway where tractor-trailer rigs are weighed periodically to check that they are not overloaded.

windshield
the window at the front of a car; *windscreen.*

yield
to let other vehicles go before you as you enter a larger road or street; *give way.*

Chapter Five
Tipping

Tipping is so important in the United States that we gave it its own little chapter.

Tips—or **gratuities**—are a large part of many people's income in the United States, so it is important not to stint on the tip when paying in restaurants, taxis, bars, etc.

In restaurants, a 15 percent tip is normal, although some people leave up to 20 percent. An easy way to figure out the tip, at least in states where the tax is around 8 percent, is to double the amount of tax, and that should make for a happy server.

Tips are expected most of the time, although if the service has not been satisfactory, customers can leave a smaller tip. If your experience was really unpleasant, you do not have to leave a tip, but make sure it was bad enough that you would never want to return to that place again, because the servers remember bad tippers.

Most restaurants do not include the gratuity in the price of a meal, although some will add 15 percent for larger groups of people. By law, a restaurant has to print any rule it has about gratuities on the menu.

In bars, it is customary to leave 10 to 15 percent of the total for the bartender. If drinks have been brought by a server, then the usual 15 percent rule applies. Of course, if you don't tip a bartender 15 percent, your drink may not be as strong as it was the first time.

For taxi drivers, the tip should be about 15 percent of the total fare.

In a hair salon or spa, tips should again be 15 percent, with $1 to $2 for any assistants. It is not necessary to tip the owner of the salon.

When staying in a hotel, it is customary to give $1 to $2 per bag to the bellhop. Hotel guests should leave $1 to $2 a day for cleaning staff. If a hotel doorman hails a cab for someone, a $1 to $2 tip is again in order.

Other people who expect tips include anyone who delivers food to someone's home, and basically anyone who provides any kind of service, with 15 percent of the total being a good rule of thumb to go by.

Do not, however, tip people such as plumbers or electricians who fix things in your home.

Chapter Six

Holidays and Vacations

🔑 Key Confusables:

British	American
bank holiday	= legal/public holiday
fancy dress	= costume
Father Christmas	= Santa Claus
holiday	= vacation
package holiday	= package tour/vacation package
travel agent's	= travel agency

🔑 Key Americanism:

Americans go on vacation, not on holiday. The word "holiday" is only used to refer to the legal holidays throughout the year. When Americans talk about "the holidays," they always mean the season that includes Hanukkah, Christmas, New Year's Day, and often Thanksgiving.

🔑 Key Grammar:

Americans say:	Americans *do not* say:
I'm going on vacation.	*I'm going on holiday.*
Happy holidays!	*Happy Christmas!*
Merry Christmas!	*Happy Christmas!*
We went to a costume party.	*We went to a fancy dress party.*

🔑 Key Cultural Points:

Americans get a lot less paid vacation time than people in Europe, with about ten days being the average. Some employees also get "personal days" they can use for whatever reason they choose. There are also nine legal holidays throughout the year. Students get a much longer summer vacation, nearly three months long, but they have fewer long breaks throughout the year.

Robins are not a symbol of Christmas to Americans.

Love Those Holidays!

Americans have a lot to learn about taking time off. Since most Americans don't get much more than two weeks of paid vacation a year, the **legal**, or **public, holidays** provide welcome breaks. Most holidays are observed on a Monday in order to give people long weekends, regardless of the day on which the actual event falls. Where you live can affect the number of holidays you have beyond the basic nine: individual states decide on any other holidays that will be observed, such as Good Friday and Columbus Day, which are not holidays in all states, and Mardi Gras, which is celebrated only in Louisiana.

Many people who work in restaurants and stores, however, still have to work on holidays, because holidays are a great excuse for sales and other events. For example, the day after Thanksgiving marks the beginning of the Christmas shopping season, and huge end-of-year sales start the day after Christmas. Shopping on these days is not a good idea if you hate crowds.

Boxing Day is not celebrated in the United States, although it is observed in Canada. Thanksgiving is celebrated in Canada, but in October.

Two uniquely American holidays are the **Fourth of July** and **Thanksgiving.** The Fourth of July celebrates the signing of the Declaration of Independence on July 4, 1776, after which there was a long war that Americans call the Revolutionary War but which still gets called the American Rebellion in Britain, for obvious reasons. The Fourth of July is an excuse for large barbecue picnics, and fireworks are lit at night.

Thanksgiving is a time for families to gather and eat a lot of food, and while they are doing this, they are supposed to remember the survival of the **Pilgrims** and their first successful harvest. It was originally celebrated with the Native Americans, without whose help the Pilgrims would probably not have survived. Thanksgiving dinner usually includes roast turkey, stuffing, cranberry sauce, and pumpkin pie. If you are a vegetarian or on a diet, you are out of luck.

Thanksgiving is always celebrated on the fourth Thursday in November, and many people take the whole weekend off work. It is one of the busiest travel weekends in the year, because many people will travel long distances to be with their families. In addition, people will open their homes to people who do not have any family celebration to go to.

It is also the occasion for the Macy's Thanksgiving Day Parade, sponsored by the famous New York City department store, which features huge balloons of many well-known cartoon characters. Many football games also take place on Thanksgiving, which sometimes inspires people to go outside for their own game of touch football.

A holiday that is still celebrated with enthusiasm in the United States is **Halloween,** on October 31. The word was originally "All Hallows' Eve," when all the spirits of the dead were thought to rise from their graves and cause problems for people before All Saints' Day (November 1). It is now celebrated by children dressing up in costumes and going **trick-or-treating** from door to door.

Carved pumpkins, or **jack-o'-lanterns,** witches, black cats, and skeletons are common decorations for the holiday. Halloween is not a legal holiday, but most people celebrate it by decorating their houses, giving candy to trick-or-treaters, or going to costume parties; schools often have parties or costume parades.

St. Valentine's Day, on February 14, is also not a legal holiday, but it is still widely celebrated. On that day, people give each other cards known as **valentines,** and other gifts such as candy and flowers. The gifts are meant to be given to someone you love in a romantic way, but children usually give valentines to all the children in their class. The pink and red decorations for Valentine's Day start appearing in stores not long after the Christmas decorations have come down.

St. Patrick's Day is on March 17, and given the large number of people who can claim Irish descent in the United States, this is usually a *pretty big event. Some cities with large Irish populations will stage parades on the day, but it also provides the average American an occasion to wear green and drink green-tinted beer. Children often pinch anyone who is not wearing green. Americans have no idea that wearing green is a political statement.*

Americans on Vacation

With the United States being one of the most affluent nations in the world, Americans are able to travel to most parts of the world, and they do. Many people will go for the organized, fourteen-European-countries-in-ten-days type of tour, in order to get the most of their limited vacation time and their investment. Remember, for Americans, more is always better.

Younger people favor the less structured, backpacking approach to travel. In fact, it has become something of a requirement to complement a college education by backpacking around Europe, almost like the Grand Tour of old.

Americans also travel quite a lot within their own country, especially on long weekend breaks or on trips based around a particular activity, such as golfing, skiing, rafting, fishing, or even shopping. National parks and other areas of natural beauty are popular destinations.

Americans also enjoy road trips and camping trips, where they can travel in their own cars or **RVs,** at their own pace and without having to depend on anyone else. Another big draw, especially for families with children, are **theme parks,** like Walt Disney World in Florida, which Americans invented and specialize in, and which provide entertainment for the whole family.

Traveling in an RV is a wildly popular thing to do, especially for couples who have retired. They sell their big houses, buy a small apartment and an RV, and travel to visit their children and "see the sights" of America they never had time to see while they were working and had two-week vacations.

School Vacations

American schoolchildren and high school and university students get more vacation time than anybody else in the United States. Schools tend to close at the end of May or early in June, and they don't open again until the end of August or early September. **Labor Day**, on the first Monday in September, traditionally marks the end of summer and the start of the school year.

All of this leaves children with up to three months out of school and not much to do. Many parents send their children to **camp**, a place that provides basic food and shelter in attractive outdoor settings. There, children can swim, hike, play sports, and do arts and crafts. Some camps are based around a particular activity, such as horseback riding, tennis, or drama. Some kids attend local **day camps**, places that organize activities for them, but in the same place where they live. Families with younger children will usually make an effort to go somewhere together during the summer, even if the children have been at camp.

Travel Arrangements

Americans use a variety of methods to organize their vacations, such as contacting **travel agencies** or going directly to the airlines or hotels by phone or on the Internet. Unless they are going somewhere very unfamiliar, Americans don't usually buy prepaid vacation packages.

· ·

Glossary of American Terms

camp
a place in the country where children spend all or part of their summer vacations. Camps have basic shelters or cabins to sleep in and organized activities. Some camps offer classes or courses for a particular activity, such as riding camp or baseball camp.

camper

1) someone attending a camp or on a camping trip. 2) a structure that fits onto a truck or that is pulled behind a vehicle, that has beds and a small kitchen in it.

Chinese New Year

a festival in late winter when Chinese Americans celebrate with fireworks and parades that feature dragons and other characters.

Cinco de Mayo

May 5, a Mexican holiday that celebrates the defeat of the French army at the Battle of Puebla in 1862. It has in recent years become a unique occasion for Mexican-American communities to celebrate their Mexican roots. It is not, as some people mistakenly believe, Mexican Independence Day.

Columbus Day

October 12, but usually observed on the second Monday in October. It celebrates Christopher Columbus's discovery of the New World in 1492.

Father's Day

the third Sunday in June, a day for honoring and celebrating fathers.

Fourth of July

the usual term for **Independence Day.**

Good Friday

the Friday before Easter, a holiday in some states.

Groundhog Day

February 2, not a legal holiday, but a popular tradition. The legend is that if a groundhog (a woodchuck) comes out of its burrow and sees its shadow, there will be six more weeks of winter. If it doesn't see its shadow, there will be an early spring.

Halloween

October 31, not a legal holiday, but widely celebrated. Children dress up in costumes and go from door to door asking for candy. People also have costume parties on that night.

Hanukkah

an annual Jewish festival that takes place in December. It celebrates the rededication to God of the Temple of Jerusalem in 165 B.C. At that time the small amount of olive oil that was needed for the rededication ceremony miraculously lasted for eight days, which is now commemorated by the lighting of one candle on each of the eight days of the festival.

holidays, the
season that includes Hanukkah, Christmas, and New Year's, and often is stretched back to include Thanksgiving. The greeting "Happy Holidays!" is often used on cards and other seasonal decorations.

Independence Day
the official name of the Fourth of July, the legal holiday that celebrates the United States' Declaration of Independence from British rule. People celebrate with parades, speeches, fireworks, and picnics and barbecues.

jack-o'-lantern
a pumpkin with a face carved on it, and a candle inside to light it up, used as a Halloween decoration.

Kwanzaa
December 26–January 1, an African-American cultural holiday that was developed in 1966 and is based on ancient African harvest celebrations. Kwanzaa takes place over a week, focusing on one particular concept each day, including faith, community, and achievement.

Labor Day
the first Monday in September and the last legal holiday of the summer. It is meant to honor working people and is celebrated with picnics and barbecues.

Martin Luther King Day
the third Monday in January, a legal holiday that celebrates the birthday of the civil rights leader.

Memorial Day
the last Monday in May. It is a day for remembering the members of the armed services killed during wartime. It usually marks the beginning of summer, and people celebrate with parades, memorial services, and the usual picnics and barbecues.

Mother's Day
the second Sunday in May, a day for honoring and celebrating mothers.

motor home

a large camper that is itself a vehicle, rather than a structure on top of a truck.

New Year's Day

January 1, a legal holiday. On New Year's Eve, December 31, people go to parties and make a lot of noise at midnight.

personal day

one of a number of days off that some companies give employees in addition to their vacation time. Personal days are often used for taking care of any business that can't be done outside of office hours.

Pilgrims

the members of the first permanent English settlement in North America, founded in 1620 by the group that arrived in what is now Plymouth, Massachusetts, aboard the *Mayflower*. They set sail for the New World from Plymouth in England.

Presidents' Day

the third Monday in February, a legal holiday that celebrates the birthdays of Abraham Lincoln (Feb. 12) and George Washington (Feb. 22).

Ramadan

the ninth month of the Islamic calendar, in late fall or early winter. It is a time for fasting and special prayers.

Rosh Hashanah

the Jewish New Year, celebrated in the autumn.

RV

a recreational vehicle, such as a camper or motor home, that people can travel in, and which provides living quarters on a trip.

spring break

a vacation period of about one week given to students in the middle of the spring school term. Widely known as a time when high school and college students go to beach resorts for unsupervised vacations.

St. Patrick's Day

March 17, when Irish Americans and anyone who claims to be Irish for the day celebrate all things Irish.

St. Valentine's Day
February 14, a day for celebrating love and friendship, usually observed by giving red and pink greeting cards, flowers, and heart-shaped candy.

Thanksgiving
the fourth Thursday in November, a legal holiday celebrating the successful first harvest in the Plymouth colony in 1621.

theme park
an elaborate amusement park based around a particular theme, character, or personality. The most famous are probably Disneyland and Walt Disney World, but other examples are Sea World, Universal Studios, and Dollywood, the brainchild of Dolly Parton.

travel agency
an agency that makes travel arrangements for customers; *travel agent's*.

trick-or-treat
to go from door to door in costume asking for treats (candy) and playing pranks on people who do not give anything.

valentine
a greeting card bearing messages of friendship or love that is given to a friend or lover.

Veterans Day
November 11, a legal holiday honoring veterans of the armed forces. Originally known as Armistice Day, to mark the end of World War I, in 1954 it was broadened in order to honor all those who have served the country in wartime.

Yom Kippur
the Day of Atonement, a Jewish holy day in the autumn marked by fasting and praying for forgiveness of sins.

Chapter Seven
Sports and Leisure

⚬┅ *Key Confusables:*

British	American
adverts	= *commercials*
American football	= *football*
cinema	= *movie theater*
cookery	= *cooking*
draughts	= *checkers*
dress circle	= *mezzanine*
film	= *movie*
football	= *soccer*
fruit machine	= *slot machine*
hockey	= *field hockey*
ice hockey	= *hockey*
interval	= *intermission*
match	= *game*
pitch	= *field*
programme	= *show/program*
racing track	= *racetrack*
side	= *team*
stalls	= *orchestra*
ten pin bowling	= *bowling*

⚬┅ *Key Americanisms:*

To Americans, their version of *football* is the only one worthy of that name. The game that is universally known as football is known as **soccer** in the United States, which is an abbreviation of its old name, *association football.*

Americans do not "support" their favorite sports teams. Instead, they *follow* a team or are *fans* of a team.

🔑 Key Grammar:

Americans say:
Tom is on the baseball team.
Let's go to the movies.
Chicago is leading 6–0.

Americans *do not* say:
Tom is in the baseball team.
Let's go to the cinema.
Chicago are leading 6–0.

🔑 Key Cultural Points:

Americans love sports, both as participants and as spectators. Sports play an important part in most people's leisure time.

While Americans can be quite fanatical about whatever sports team they happen to be loyal to, it doesn't usually lead to the outbreaks of violence that happen in some other countries.

There is relatively little awareness or coverage of international sports.

· ·

Leisure Time

With the United States being such a large and diverse country, there are pastimes and leisure activities to suit everyone. However, sports—for both spectators and participants—are a major part of most people's lives. Among the most popular of spectator sports are three that are almost unique to the United States—baseball, **football,** and basketball.

Speaking of Baseball

Baseball, the national game, besides being incredibly popular, has contributed a number of words and phrases that have become a part of the language. For example, someone might say that a person who has attempted something and failed has *struck out*. A *ballpark figure* is an approximate number. If someone *gets to first base* they succeed at the first step of something they are trying to do. This expression is also used to mean that someone has succeeded in kissing someone they are interested in sexually. A *pinch hitter* is someone who steps in for another person in an emergency.

Many children play baseball either at school or in **Little League**, a national organization of baseball and **softball** teams for children. Baseball is also played in colleges and universities. Outstanding college players often go on to play professionally. Adults also play baseball for fun, sometimes with colleagues from work, or against a team from a rival company. There are also organized amateur baseball leagues around the country.

In terms of professional teams, there are two basic divisions, the **major** and the **minor leagues.** The major leagues include the American and the National Leagues. The season lasts from April to October and the championship, or **World Series**, is played between the champion teams from each league.

The baseball championship is the World Series, even though the only international teams that play in the American baseball leagues are Canadian. The basketball championship is the World Championship, even though, again, the only non–U.S. teams play in Canada.

Football

The game known as football in the United States is not at all like the game known as football in most other parts of the world. Originally, it was similar to rugby football, which is where the name came from. It's played by two teams of eleven players, most of them very large men, wearing protective equipment that makes them look even bigger.

Football is played by organized teams in schools, usually starting in junior high school and high school, where being on a sports team gives a kid a higher social status. College football is a popular spectator sport and a huge source of income for colleges and universities, due to sponsorship deals and TV broadcasting revenues. The college football season ends around New Year's Day with **bowl games** played by the best teams from around the country.

Professional football is played by the teams of the National Football League (NFL) in a season that runs from late summer to January. The championship is called the **Super Bowl.**

While rugby is sometimes played in the United States, it is probably the only former British colony where cricket has made no impact whatsoever. Americans have baseball, after all.

Basketball

Basketball is one of the most popular and exciting of spectator sports, as well as being a favorite leisure game for many people since it requires little equipment besides a ball and a net, called a **basket.** Basketball courts are found in many parks and public spaces. Basketball has become one of the biggest and most lucrative professional sports, with top players earning huge amounts of money both for playing and for endorsing products such as sports shoes.

The professional basketball organization is the National Basketball Association (NBA), which holds its annual championship, the **World Championship** (or NBA Finals), early each summer. College basketball is equally popular and gets just as much television coverage as professional games. The **NCAA** college basketball tournament (March Madness, or the Final Four) is played each spring.

Other Sports

Americans enjoy many other sports—golf, tennis, skiing, swimming, and cycling, just to name a few—and there are many public facilities for doing all of them. **Soccer** has become increasingly popular in recent years, especially among children and teenagers, although it has not gained as much acceptance on a professional level. Hockey is another favorite sport, and its popularity is not limited to the colder, northern states.

"Hockey" always refers to the sport played on ice. Field hockey is not very common and is played primarily by young women in schools.

Bowling is a recreational sport that is popular with people of all ages across the country. **Bowling alleys** can be found everywhere, and each game costs only a couple of dollars. Many people play in organized amateur leagues, or have a regular bowling night. However, most Americans go bowling only occasionally.

Lawn bowling, or bowls, and crown green bowling are not commonly played in the United States.

Skating continues to be very popular, especially in-line skating (better known as "rollerblading," after the trademark Rollerblade **in-line skates**). It's not uncommon to see people skating down streets and sidewalks, or on special paths in parks and along urban lakes and waterfronts. In-line skating has largely replaced roller skating (on four-wheeled skates), but there are still **roller rinks** where you can skate indoors and listen to music. **Ice rinks** are widely available for ice skaters, and people also skate on frozen lakes and ponds in the winter.

Fitness Freaks

Although there are many severely overweight Americans, there are just as many who regularly do some kind of exercise. In this land where people will not walk to the store, walking as a form of exercise is incredibly popular in all its forms, from casual strolling to intense **power walking.** Jogging and running are other popular and inexpensive forms of exercise.

Gyms and health clubs are found everywhere. They can be quite affordable, so many people have memberships, which they probably don't use as often as they intended to when they first joined. However, the people who do go regularly tend to talk about the time they spend in the gym with an almost religious zeal.

Television

It's sad to say, but watching television has become one of the most popular national pastimes. Originally there were only three national television **networks,** which broadcast around the country through local **affiliates.** There are more networks now, but the original three—ABC, NBC, and CBS, or the Big Three—remain the most powerful and most viewed. These are all commercial networks that earn their money from advertising. Because of the commercial nature of American television, the **Nielsen ratings** are crucial. Any show that doesn't perform well in the ratings is almost immediately dropped.

Another national network, the Public Broadcasting System (PBS), is not commercial and depends on viewer contributions and corporate sponsorship to stay in business. PBS channels are known for educational and arts programming, and for showing programs from the U.K. The major networks usually broadcast on VHF (Very High Frequency).

There are also many independent local stations around the country. They tend to have specialized programming, such as old movies, religious programs, community interest, or a mix of all of these, and often broadcast on UHF (Ultra High Frequency).

If that doesn't seem like enough choice, cable television provides many more channels, including premium movie channels and **pay-per-view** access. Most cable channels provide programming of a specific type (old movies, cartoons), or targeted at a specific audience (women, children, Spanish speakers, etc.). Cable television is not subject to the same regulations as network television, so cable companies can broadcast programs that contain violence, sex, and obscene language, which is usually carefully avoided in network programming.

There are around seven channels that are available for free, although you have to put up with a lot of advertising on all but PBS. There is no annual fee for television service. Cable service, however, has a basic monthly fee, and costs even more for special channels that show major films. Satellite service is also available, although it is not as common.

Radio

There are thousands of local radio stations across the country catering to every taste. Besides broadcasting every possible category of music, there are also many stations devoted to talk shows that cover a wide variety of topics. There are not many radio networks, although National Public Radio, or NPR (the radio equivalent of PBS), broadcasts across the country and specializes in news, current events, and more cultural programming than the average radio station. Most radio stations are commercial, although there are some advertising-free stations run by universities, colleges, and other public institutions.

Americans listen to the radio most when they are driving. **Drive-time** programs are broadcast during the daily rush hour periods.

Movies and Theaters

Watching movies is another very popular leisure activity, both at home on video and TV, and at **movie theaters.** Movie tickets are not very expensive, with tickets costing between $5 and $10 (prices are highest in large cities like Los Angeles and New York). Movie theaters and **multiplexes** also offer a variety of discounts, such as reduced prices before a certain time or on a particular day.

There are also discount theaters that show movies that have already played at regular theaters (first-run theaters) for a while. Admission to these second-run theatres is only about $1 to $2. Some cities also have **revival** or art movie theaters, which specialize in foreign and art films, as well as classic old movies.

Most Americans use the word "movie" when talking about a film, although "film" is also used, especially when referring to the medium itself. The word "cinema" is also used in this context, or in the names of some theaters, but the place where movies are shown is a **movie the-ater** *or* **movie house.** *Americans usually say they are "going to the movies," rather than saying they are going to the movie theater. Movie tickets all cost the same price in a theater (although prices may be lower for children or senior citizens); there are no cheaper seats.*

The American movie rating system is as follows:

G	general audience—appropriate for all audiences
PG	"parental guidance"—parents may not want children to see the movie
PG-13	parental guidance is suggested for children under the age of thirteen
R	restricted—no one under seventeen is admitted unless a parent or guardian is with them
NC-17	no children under seventeen are admitted

Movie theaters may ask for proof of age if someone looks too young for a particular movie.

On and Off Broadway

The United States has a thriving theater scene, from the latest shows on Broadway in New York to amateur and professional productions in towns across the country. Many Broadway shows have touring companies, which bring the big shows to theaters in many major cities. These touring plays are of the same quality as the Broadway shows, although the big stars don't always go on tour. If a play is successful and popular enough, there may also be an extended run in Los Angeles or Chicago, but New York remains the center of the theater world.

When buying theater tickets, keep in mind that the different seating areas have different names in American English. The best seats are in the **orchestra,** *which is the area around the stage and orchestra pit. The first balcony is known as the* **mezzanine.** *The gallery is never referred to as "the gods."*

Gambling

Most forms of gambling are illegal in most states, with the exception of Nevada and New Jersey, home to, respectively, Las Vegas and Atlantic City. Gambling casinos can also be found on Mississippi riverboats and on Native American reservations, which are exempt from state gambling laws. These casinos have proven to be a great source of income for the tribes that operate them.

Casinos in the United States are not the elegant establishments they are in other countries, and they do not generally have a strict dress code. The people who go to casinos or other gambling places are not referred to as "punters." Coin-operated gambling machines are called **slot machines**.

Betting on horse racing and greyhound racing is legal at **racetracks** around the country. Off-track betting (OTB) is illegal everywhere except Connecticut, Nevada, and New York. Gambling on other sports is allowed only in Oregon and Nevada.

Many states have lotteries, played the traditional way or with **scratch cards.** There is no national lottery.

• •

Glossary of American Terms

affiliate
a local TV station that broadcasts the programs produced by one of the national networks along with some locally produced shows.

athletics
sports in general. ➪ **track (and field).**

baseball
a game similar to what is known in Britain as *rounders,* played by two teams of nine players. The two teams alternately play at bat or on the field. The **pitcher** for the team on the field pitches the ball to the **batter,** who attempts to hit it and then run around the four bases in order to score.

basket

the round metal hoop with a net attached to it that a ball is thrown through to score points in basketball. A basket is also the score itself—this is not usually called a *goal* except in the term **field goal.**

batter

in baseball, the player who tries to hit the ball with a bat.

bowl game

one of a number of football games played on or around January 1 that the best college teams are invited to play in. There is no single winning college football team because there are so many of them around the country and they play in different regional conferences.

bowling

an indoor game in which a player attempts to knock down ten pins by rolling a heavy ball down a wooden lane.

bowling alley

a place with many lanes for bowling. Bowling alleys rent shoes and balls, and usually sell food and drinks.

call letters

the four-letter code assigned to radio or television stations. The codes start with either a "K" or a "W." "K" indicates that a station is located west of the Mississippi, while a "W" means that it is located to the east.

commercial

an advertisement played on the radio or on television; *advert.*

diamond

a baseball field, so called because of the diamond shape made by the placement of the four bases.

down

in football, one of four plays that a team gets in which they attempt to move the ball at least ten yards toward the opponent's goal. If they gain ten yards, they retain the ball and get another four downs.

draft

a system by which professional teams get to pick new players from college and amateur sports programs.

drive-time
radio broadcasting during rush hour periods, when people usually listen to the radio in their cars.

end zone
in football, the area at either end of a football field from the goal line to the end of the field. The goalposts are located in this area.

field goal
in football, a score of three points made by kicking the ball between the goalposts. In basketball, a field goal is a score of two points obtained by throwing the ball through the basket from the court during regular play. A score of three points is obtained if the ball is thrown from beyond a specified distance.

football
a game that is somewhat similar to rugby, but players wear helmets and heavily padded uniforms. The object of the game is to move the ball across the opponent's goal line, advancing in a series of plays known as **downs.** The ball may be carried, passed, or kicked down the field. There are eleven players per team on the field.

franchise
a professional sports team. Franchises have owners who may sell the team or move it to a different city if they do not like the way a city hosts its team.

gridiron
a football field, so called because of the pattern of lines marked out on it.

home run, homer
a play in baseball in which the batter hits the ball out of the playing field so that he can run around all of the bases and score a run.

ice rink, ice skating rink
a place where people can ice skate indoors that rents skates.

infield
the part of a baseball field within the diamond formed by the four bases.

in-line skates
boots with a single row of wheels underneath, like ice skates only with wheels.

intermission
the time period between acts of a play; *interval*.

Little League
a program of organized baseball and softball for children between the ages of eight and twelve.

major leagues
also called "the majors"; the two main national groups of professional baseball teams (the American League and the National League).

mezzanine
the lowest balcony in a theater, or the seats on that balcony; *dress circle*.

minor leagues
a group of professional baseball teams that are not part of the major leagues. Many major league clubs operate minor league teams, which provide the opportunity for players to play and develop until they are ready to play in the major leagues.

movie theater
a place where movies are shown; *cinema*.

multiplex
a large movie theater complex with many theaters in one building.

MVP
Most Valuable Player; a title given to the best player of a game or a championship in most professional and college sports.

NCAA
National Collegiate Athletic Association; the association that includes over one thousand colleges and universities and that regulates college sports.

network
a television company that produces programs that are then broadcast by all the local TV stations affiliated with the network. The major American TV networks are ABC (American Broadcast-

ing Companies), NBC (National Broadcasting Company), CBS (Columbia Broadcasting System), Fox, WB (Warner Brothers), UPN (United Paramount Network), and PBS (Public Broadcasting System).

Nielsen ratings
the rating system that television broadcasters use to find out how many households are watching a particular program.

orchestra
the area of a theater closest to the stage; *stalls*.

outfield
the part of a baseball field outside the diamond formed by the four bases.

pay-per-view
programs on cable television that cost extra to watch each time. These are usually special movies or sports programs, such as major boxing matches.

pickup game
an informal basketball game played with whoever happens to be around a public court.

pitcher
in baseball, the player who throws the ball to the batter.

play-offs
a series of games played to decide a sports championship. The term is used in most sports.

power walking
a form of exercise that consists of walking very fast and pumping the arms back and forth.

punt
in football, to kick the ball by dropping it from the hands and kicking it before it hits the ground. A **punter** is someone who does this, and not a customer or someone who gambles.

quarterback
the player on a football team who calls the signals for the plays. He receives the ball from the center, then either passes the ball down the field, hands off to another player who will run with the ball, or runs with the ball himself.

rerun

a television show that is broadcast again after its original broadcast; *repeat*.

revival theater

a movie theater that plays older, classic movies or foreign films.

roller rink, roller skating rink

a place where people can roller-skate indoors that rents skates.

run

a complete circuit of the four bases in baseball, worth one point (one run).

scratch card

a lottery game card. You scratch the surface off the card to see if you have won any money.

slot machine

a coin-operated gambling machine; *fruit machine*.

softball

a game like baseball that is played on a smaller diamond, with a larger, softer ball that is pitched underhand.

Stanley Cup

the National Hockey League championship.

strike

in baseball, a failed attempt by the batter to hit the ball pitched to him, a hit into an illegal area, or a pitch within a specific area that a batter does not hit. Batters are allowed three strikes before being called out.

Super Bowl

the game played between the winning American and National Football Conference teams to decide the National Football League championship. The game is traditionally played on the last Sunday in January and is probably the biggest sports event in the United States.

tackle

in football, to pull an opponent down to the ground so that he cannot carry the ball any farther.

tip-off
the action that starts a basketball game. The official throws the ball up between two players from opposing teams who jump and try to tap the ball toward their teammates.

touchdown
in football, the act of successfully crossing the opponent's goal line, scoring six points.

touch football
a form of football played without the protective uniforms in which the person carrying the ball can be stopped when he is touched by a member of the opposite team, rather than being tackled.

track (and field)
sports that involve running, jumping, throwing, etc.; *athletics.*

World Championship
the series of games played to decide the National Basketball Association's championship. The NBA Finals are usually played early in the summer.

World Series
the major league baseball championship, played between the winning American and National League teams. The World Series is played early in the fall.

Chapter Eight
American Education

⌐ Key Confusables:

British	American
degree course	= *major*
education authority	= *school district*
form	= *grade*
grounds	= *campus*
mark	= *grade*
postgraduate	= *graduate*
primary school	= *elementary school*
public school	= *private school*
reception class	= *kindergarten*
revise	= *review*
secondary school	= *junior high and high school*
term	= *quarter* or *semester*
year	= *grade*

⌐ Key Americanisms:

In high schools and universities, the years have names:

freshman	= first-year student
sophomore	= second-year student
junior	= third-year student
senior	= fourth-year student

School can refer to any type of educational institution, not just to primary and secondary school.

⌐ Key Grammar:

Americans tend to use the terms *college* and *university* interchangeably. However, *college*, rather than *university*, is used as the uncountable noun in American English.

Americans say:	**Americans _do not_ say:**
I went to college in 1990.	_I was at college in 1990._
I'm in college.	_I'm at college._
I went to Ohio State University.	_I went to university at Ohio State._
I went to college at Ohio State.	

⚷ Key Cultural Points:

Americans don't specialize in a subject until fairly late, often not until their last two years at a college or university. They figure, if you want to specialize, get a master's degree. Therefore, a bachelor's degree from an American institution does not generally represent the same degree of specialized knowledge in a subject area that bachelor's degrees from other countries represent.

Americans are very competitive in school, both in academics and in sports.

••••••••••••••••••••••••••••

The primary goal of the American high school and college education is not mainly to produce brilliantly educated people with narrow, specialized skills. Rather, it's to produce broadly educated people who can contribute to society by getting a job. Anyone who successfully completes the twelve years of required primary and secondary education will receive a **high school diploma.** Although in most states education is not required after the age of sixteen, not having this qualification makes any further education or decently paid employment almost impossible.

The American system of **grading,** known outside the United States as "continuous assessment," looks at the whole of a student's performance and encourages competitiveness, communication, and individuality, all qualities that are highly valued by U.S. society (⇨ **_Grading and Exams_** on page 122.)

Public vs. Private

Primary and secondary education is free and available to every-one in the United States, although there is also an extensive sys-tem of private and **parochial** schools in the country. There is also a growing number of families who, mostly for religious rea-sons, choose to educate their children at home (a practice called "home schooling"). The majority of American schoolchildren attend free **public schools,** however.

It is the individual states, rather than the federal government, that are responsible for education; therefore, there is not a national curriculum that all schools must follow. The day-to-day running of schools is supervised by the local **school district.** School districts cover a geographic area within larger cities, or cover an entire small town or rural community. Funding for schools comes from state and local governments and local taxes within each school district. This means, in general, that rich areas have well-funded schools and poor areas have schools with few resources. So much for American equality!

The American **public school** *is funded by the government and is free to all children. The American* **private school**, *for which* **tuition** *fees are charged, is roughly equivalent to the British public school.*

The American **prep(aratory) school** *is usually a private school, typically a high school but sometimes including the lower grades. These are also called "academies," and are known for high standards of education.*

The School Year

The school year usually starts in early September and runs through to early or mid-June. Generally, 180 days of class time are required by law; in some places, the school year may be extended for a few days to make up for any days lost during the year due to bad weather that temporarily closed the school.

School years are typically divided into two **semesters**, which may be further divided into **quarters.**

Apart from summer vacation, children also get one to two weeks off at the end of December and during the spring, as well as all the national holidays (➪ **School Vacations** on page 88).

Colleges and universities are divided either into **quarters** (sometimes called "trimesters") or **semesters.** In the quarter system, the school year is three periods of roughly ten weeks—fall, winter, and spring—with a summer quarter offered but not required. In the semester system, there are two semesters of roughly fourteen weeks, usually with a break for the month of January, when optional short classes are offered.

Elementary School

Schooling starts officially at about age five or six, with **elementary school**, also known as **grade school.** Before elementary school, children can attend a year or more of optional early education, including **preschool/nursery school** and **kindergarten.** Preschool is for children between the ages of three and four, and is a way of easing children into the whole routine of school from an early age. In kindergarten, five-year-olds learn early reading and number skills, and develop some of the social and practical skills they will need when they start elementary school.

Elementary school consists of five to six years of basic education including reading, writing, arithmetic, social studies, science, physical education (usually referred to as **PE** or **gym** class), music, and art. American schooling is divided into **grades,** with one grade being completed per year, starting with first grade and going up to twelfth grade, the last year of secondary school.

Students in each grade are referred to as **first graders, second graders, fifth graders,** *etc., not "grade ones" or "year ones." Keep in mind, too, that they are usually called "students" not "pupils."*

Middle School/Junior High School

When students finish fifth or sixth grade, at the age of about eleven or twelve, they move on to either **middle school** or **junior high school**, depending on which system their school district uses. This part of the education system is a sort of stepping stone between elementary and high school and lasts for two or three years.

A major difference between elementary school and junior high or middle school is that students start to change classes, going to different classrooms with different teachers for each subject. Before this stage, students usually stay in just one main classroom, only going elsewhere for classes such as PE or art.

High School

The next step is **high school**, typically a four-year program that starts with ninth grade and ends with twelfth grade. Students start high school at about age fourteen. In high school, students have to complete a program of general education courses, but they will also be allowed to choose a series of **electives**, in more specialized subjects such as computer science, music, art, and foreign languages.

Students in each year of high school are referred to by a special term for each grade. Ninth graders are **freshmen**; *tenth graders are* **sophomores**; *eleventh graders are* **juniors**, *and twelfth graders are* **seniors**. *These terms are also applied to students in four-year colleges and universities.*

Since, as we said, the end goal of American education is to produce well-rounded, broadly educated individuals who can function productively in society, academic achievement is not the only measure of success in school. Students are encouraged to participate in **extracurricular activities** such as sports, student government, drama clubs, and debate teams. All of these things are also considered when someone is applying for college admission or even for a job. Many of these activities allow students to learn valuable lessons in leadership, teamwork, and effective communication.

Higher Education

A **college education** is almost indispensable for any sort of professional career. After getting a high school education, practically anybody can go to a college or university. There are over three thousand colleges and universities in the United States, all with differing entrance requirements, tuition fees, and course specialties. They also come in many different sizes, from the vast state universities, with enrollment in the tens of thousands, to small private colleges with fewer than one thousand students.

College usually refers to a higher education institution that offers a four-year program and grants only bachelor's degrees. It can be independent, or it can be part of a university. A **university** is usually a larger institution, often made up of specialized schools or colleges, that grants graduate degrees as well as bachelor's degrees. However, Americans say that they are "in college" no matter which type of institution they attend.

Americans will rarely say they were "at university"; they're more likely to say "I went to X university/college." When they talk about their early education, they will also be more specific and say they went to grade school, middle school, or high school at a particular school.

Getting Accepted

Once a student chooses a few likely colleges, the application process can begin. A college application gives details of a student's academic record and also covers the extracurricular activities and volunteer organizations a student may have participated in, any honors received, and even any part-time jobs he or she may have held. Therefore, it really helps to have more on one's application than just good grades.

The reason for this is, again, that Americans value well-rounded people. If you have an excellent academic record but few other activities to your credit, it's taken as evidence that you have spent the better part of your life studying and not doing much else.

Colleges and universities will also look at a student's college entrance exam scores (➡ *Grading and Exams* on page 122). The college's **catalog** (a prospectus) will tell you the minimum scores necessary for admission. Many colleges will also ask a potential student to come in for an interview before offering admission.

*Because the quality of a high school education varies so much from district to district, colleges will often require new students to take basic English and math tests the week before they start classes. If you do not pass one of these tests, you are required to take a **remedial** course until you are skilled enough to pass the test. These courses are offered at the college or university, but you'll pay tuition for them.*

Americans do not talk about getting a college "place." They say they have been "accepted to" a college.

Earning Your Degree

After being accepted to a university or college, students are free to choose any course of study they want. They rarely have to compete for a limited number of places. It is usually not necessary for students to decide immediately what subject they will study. In fact, it is not unknown for a student in the third year of college to still be undecided. However, a student will usually select a **major**—the major field of study—relatively early on.

To earn a degree in a subject, a student must complete a fixed number of required and elective courses, measured in **credits** or **units** (➡ *Grading and Exams* on page 122). Before moving into the more specialized classes in their chosen subject, students are often required to complete a number of general education courses in subjects such as English, science, history, and foreign languages. However, it is up to the individual student to take any required classes; the school will provide guidelines, but it is the student's responsibility to actually sign up for and pass all courses.

Students may also pick a **minor,** or a second subject that interests them, which may or may not be related to their major. Again, there are certain required courses that must be completed in order to meet the requirements for a minor. A student may also work on a **double major**, meeting the major requirements for two subjects.

Undergraduate students attend classes on a regular basis, usually two or three times a week for each subject. The instructor will give lectures on the subject, and students are responsible for knowing the material covered. They will be tested several times in the course of a quarter or semester, usually in a **midterm** and a **final exam.** There may also be written assignments or research projects to complete for the final grade.

Students may seek **tutors** *for extra help in subjects that they are having trouble in. Tutors are usually more advanced students or graduate students who do this as a way of supplementing their income. They are not official employees of the college or university.*

Students go to classes, not to lectures. A lecture is a special presentation by a guest speaker, and is open to all the students at a university. Classes are open only to students who have signed up and paid for them.

Once a student has completed all the necessary coursework, and passed the classes with a high enough grade, he or she is eligible for a **bachelor's degree**—either a **Bachelor of Arts (B.A.)** or a **Bachelor of Science (B.S.)** degree. It usually takes four years to finish an **undergraduate** degree, although many students take longer because they need to work to pay **tuition.**

Junior/Community College

An alternative to four-year institutions is the **junior** or **community college**, an institution that offers two-year degree programs in general or technical education. Students who complete the course of study at a community or junior college earn an **associate's degree (A.A.)** in either the arts or sciences. These colleges are also much less expensive to attend than four-year colleges.

Students are often part-time, or they may be older people returning to school or working on a new qualification when returning to work. Many students transfer to a four-year institution after receiving an associate degree, as a way of completing their general education requirements more cheaply.

Graduate Studies

After earning a bachelor's degree, a student can go on to graduate school to work on a **master's degree (M.A.).** This usually takes one or two years of further studies. Many students will start work on a master's degree after they have been working for a while; a master's degree has almost become a requirement for advancement in many careers, so it has become more common for people to get a higher degree.

A master's degree can be followed by a **doctorate**, or **Ph.D.**, which requires up to four more years of study, plus a **dissertation** (a doctoral thesis).

The course of study for a Ph.D. is not the same type of course as that for a D.Phil. The American doctorate is a combination of taught courses, exams, and a dissertation.

Financing

The one very real question that determines whether someone can go to college is whether they can afford it. Since all colleges and universities, even those run by the states, charge tuition and fees, a student has to pay anywhere between $2,000 and $35,000 per year to attend a four-year college. The total will depend on what type of college a student chooses: publicly funded state universities are the less expensive option, and private colleges are the most expensive. Among private institutions, the most prestigious and exclusive schools, such as those of the **Ivy League**, top the list.

Help!

Since a college education has become so necessary for getting ahead, many parents will scrimp, save, and sacrifice in order to send their children to college, often starting savings or investment accounts for that purpose as soon as their children are born. This doesn't mean, however, that those without financial means can't go to college. There is a wide variety of scholarships, student loans, and other forms of **financial aid** that students can apply for to help finance their education.

Financial aid from government sources is need-based. Families must provide details of their finances to prove that they qualify for aid. **Scholarships** are more broadly available to students with a variety of qualifications—for example, an excellent academic record, musical ability, or athletic talent. Athletic skill is particularly important in universities where sports such as basketball and football bring in a lot of money. Universities are happy to pay tuition and **room and board** fees for students who can make a difference to the school's sports program.

The **student loan** is another option available to students. Low-interest loans, repayable after graduation, are available from a number of government and private organizations. The amount that a student can borrow varies from case to case, and is determined when an application is made. **Grants** are another type of financial aid for students; they are usually given to students working in a particular field or at a particular college. The big advantage of the grant is that it does not have to be paid back.

Work-study programs are a way for a student to earn money while working for the school or college, or for local companies. Part of the student's wages are paid for with government funds, which makes student workers more attractive to businesses. Work-study doesn't usually cover all of a student's tuition and **fees,** but it does make employment at better wages more likely. Many American students have part-time jobs, whether work-study or not. Of course, all this work experience comes in handy when applying for jobs after college.

Student Life

Many young people will leave home when they finish high school and go away to college. However, just as many will stay at home and attend a local college or university. The students who go away will have several options open to them in terms of living arrangements.

Dorms and Apartments

The simplest living option is a room in a university-run student dormitory, or **dorm,** which is a large building where hundreds of other students live. It is quite common to have a **roommate.**

*The word **roommate** is used for the person you share a room with, as well as someone you share a house or apartment with.*

Dorms can be single-sex or **coed** (mixed), and will have rules about **curfews** and guests, especially for students in their first years of college. Despite the restrictions, dorm life provides a young person's first taste of freedom and independence, away from their parents. Students who live in dorms do not usually cook for themselves, since the fees for **on-campus** living nearly always include meals at the student cafeteria. It is not unusual, though, to find a small refrigerator or microwave oven in a dorm room, and nearly every student has an electric popcorn popper.

You'll nearly always smell popcorn popping somewhere in a dorm. It's a favorite snack food for college students, and it provides fuel for the *all-night study sessions known as **all-nighters**. If a student has to stay up all night preparing for a test or writing an essay, they **pull an all-nighter**.*

Another living option is to rent an apartment near the university campus. This is usually done with one or two other students and is probably the most expensive alternative, although it does mean that a student is completely independent. Some universities also own apartments for students to use.

Not Quite Independent

During their undergraduate years, students often go back to their parents' homes, especially for holidays such as Thanksgiving and Christmas. If students go to school in the same state their parents live in, they are also likely to go home on weekends, often to do their laundry and get a home-cooked meal. Students whose families live far away will often be invited to the homes of students whose parents are closer, especially for Thanksgiving.

Greeks

Students may also live in a **fraternity** or **sorority** house. Fraternities and sororities are single-sex social organizations that have names that are represented by two or three Greek letters—hence, members are often known as **Greeks**—such as Chi Omega, Sigma Tau Alpha, and Kappa Alpha. Sorority and fraternity members tend to socialize only within the Greek system, and for this reason are viewed as something of an elitist minority.

To live in a Greek house, a student must become a member of one of these societies. They have strict rules for admission, often requiring new students to be referred by a former member. There is a period known as **rush,** usually at the beginning of the academic year, when a lot of parties and other social events take place. This gives potential members a chance to meet existing members and decide which fraternity or sorority they want to join, or **pledge.**

Once students have been accepted, they will usually move into the organization's house, which may offer a slightly higher standard of accommodation, as well as better food, than the student dorms. Living in a Greek house can be more expensive than living in a dorm, and there are rules about curfews and visiting hours for the house as well. Many houses require their members to maintain a particular **GPA** (⇨ *Grading and Exams,* below).

Grading and Exams

From the time American children start school to the time they graduate from high school, they almost never have to take any one formal examination that determines whether they move on to the next grade or level. Rather, academic performance is evaluated on many different aspects of a student's performance. A grade in a subject will depend on test scores, homework assignments, and class participation.

This means that students have more than just one chance to prove themselves, and if they are not at their best when taking exams, they won't necessarily fail. Because this system is the only one that Americans know, they don't use the term "continual assessment" to describe it, and they think the examination system in most other countries is incredibly unfair.

The word **grade** *is used where British English would use "mark," which is rarely used in American English. Students are given a particular grade on a test or assignment, or in a class; a teacher grades papers. Very often, a* **score** *(usually a percentage out of 100) is given on a test or assignment, which is then converted to an equivalent letter grade.*

Get Out Your Calculator

Grading begins in earnest at the middle school level, and is usually done with letters from A to F, with A being "excellent"; B "good"; C "average"; D "poor"; and F "failed." The letter E is not used in the grading scale. The grades may be further qualified by the use of the symbols "+" and "–" after the letters, so that A+ is the very best grade one can get, and a D– could be a very poor, but passing, grade. A scale of 1 to 100 is also used sometimes, but the number would be converted to a letter to assign the student a grade. An A grade corresponds roughly to a score of 100 to 90; B is 89 to 80; C is 79 to 70; D is 69 to 60; and F is anything below that.

At the end of every quarter, students receive an overall grade that is an average of all the individual grades they got on assignments and tests during the quarter. At the end of each semester, the two quarter grades are averaged to produce the grade that becomes part of a student's **grade point average**, or **GPA.**

The GPA is an average taken of all of a student's semester grades that assigns a numerical value to each letter grade on a scale from 0 to 4.0: An A grade is 4.0, a B is 3.0, a C is 2.0, and a D is 1.0. A final university GPA of 3.5 or above is roughly equivalent to a British honors degree. Students with a GPA of 3.5 or higher graduate **cum laude** (with honor); 3.7 or higher is **magna cum laude** (with great honor); 3.9 or higher is **summa cum laude** (with highest honor).

College Credits

Obviously, you have to have some math skills to figure out the American grading system. But it's not over yet. In order to complete a college or university degree, you have to get enough **credits** or **units** to graduate.

A credit is roughly equal to one hour of class time. A typical college class will meet for three or five hours per week. In the quarter system (⇨ **The School Year** on page 112), a student earns three or five **credits** every quarter for a three- or five-hour class. The usual full-time student takes fifteen hours of classes per quarter, and 180 credits are required to graduate. In the semester system, the word **unit** is usually used, and each semester-long class also earns units that relate to the number of hours of class time.

Roughly half of a student's college credits must be earned in required classes that cover all general areas of study, and the other half is used for the student's **major** and any **minor** or elective courses.

Finally, just passing the courses often isn't enough to graduate; in many universities, there is a minimum GPA that must be earned, and the minimum is often higher for courses in the student's major.

Okay, There Are a Couple of Major Exams

Although exams are rarely required to move from one grade to the next, students who are planning to go to college after high school will have to take one of the national standardized college entrance exams—the **ACT** or the **SAT.** These tests are conducted nationally on fixed dates during the school year.

The general test assesses students' aptitude in verbal and mathematical skills rather than evaluating their knowledge of any specific subject, so that studying for it is more a question of completing sample tests to learn strategies than it is of learning facts. There is also a range of specialized tests in specific subjects; these are not required, but can often make a difference in a student's acceptance to a preferred university. Students can take the exams repeatedly until they achieve the scores they want.

A different set of optional exams, called **Advanced Placement** exams, are a means for students to **place out** of some of the compulsory subjects at a university, such as English composition, algebra, or foreign languages. A good score on an AP exam proves a certain level of knowledge of a given subject, so that the student does not have to take any basic courses in that subject. The AP exams are the closest American equivalent to British A levels. High schools often provide AP courses for college-bound students.

To be accepted into a graduate study program, students must take the **GRE** after completing a bachelor's degree (or in their senior year). This is also a general exam that tests verbal and mathematical skills. Some graduate programs, such as law and medical schools, have specialized national exams.

••••••••••••••••••••••••••••••••

Glossary of American Terms

ACT

American College Test; one of the standardized college entrance tests that American students take before applying to college. Some colleges and universities prefer this test to the **SAT.**

adjunct professor

a professor at a college or university who is not a full, permanent member of the faculty.

all-nighter

when a student stays up all night to finish an essay or study for a test.

AP test

Advanced Placement test; a standardized national test in a specific subject taken by a college-bound high school student. AP tests are not required for college entrance, but the more elite universities expect applicants to have taken AP courses and tests. Passing an AP test can give a student college credit in that subject.

assembly

an occasion when all the students in a school meet together in a large auditorium, usually the school's gym. At assemblies, students can hear special speakers, listen to concerts by school music groups, or learn new cheers for their sports teams.

assistant professor

the third highest rank in the faculty at a college or university, below **associate professor** and above **instructor.**

associate professor

the second highest rank in the faculty at a college or university, below **professor** and above **assistant professor.**

associate's degree

the degree earned at a junior or community college, usually after two years of study; also called an **A.A.**

baccalaureate
a religious service for the graduating class of a high school, college, or university, held shortly before commencement; also a bachelor's degree.

bachelor's degree
the degree earned at a four-year college or university; also called a **B.A.** (in the arts) or a **B.S.** (in the sciences).

blue book
a small booklet containing blank pages, used for taking essay-type exams in high school or college.

cafeteria
the school or college *canteen.*

campus
the land and buildings that make up a school, college, or university. The terms **on-campus** and **off-campus** are used to talk about where students live or work.

cheer
a short rhyme with a strong rhythm that is chanted loudly by people attending sports games and competitions, as a way of supporting their team.

cheerleader
a high school or college student who is part of a cheerleading squad. Cheerleaders do dancelike movements and acrobatics to the rhythm of the cheers.

cheerleading squad
also called **cheer squad.** A small, select group of students who lead the crowds in organized cheering at sports games and competitions.

class ring
a ring that students can buy with their high school or college symbol and initials on it, as well as the year of their graduation.

commencement
the yearly ceremony at which new graduates receive their diplomas, and special awards are given out.

counselor
a school or college official who gives students advice on aca-

demic and career matters. Some schools also have psychological counselors who offer help to students with personal problems.

credit

a unit of measurement that gives a value to each course a college student takes, according to the number of hours of class time the course requires. A student must earn a particular number of credits in a special subject to major in that subject, and must also have a specific number of credits to graduate. Also called "hour" or **unit.**

curfew

a rule about how late a student can return to a dorm at night, or how late guests may stay in a dorm room.

cut school/cut class

to not attend school or a particular class, especially to do something that might be considered more fun than studying.

dean

an administrative officer in charge of a college or school within a university, for example the Dean of Arts and Sciences. A dean is usually a professor as well.

dean's list

a list of the students with the highest grades in a college or university, usually announced every semester or quarter.

detention

a punishment given to a student who misbehaves, which consists of having to stay after school for a certain amount of time, or coming in to school on a Saturday, usually to do schoolwork.

diploma

a document that proves that a student has completed high school, college, or a graduate degree. Some technical training courses also give diplomas.

dissertation

the research thesis, often three hundred pages or more, that is one of the requirements for students to earn a **Ph.D.**

doctorate

a doctor's degree. This term usually refers to a **Ph.D.**, but can also be used for other doctor's degrees, such as an **M.D.** (medical doctor) or **J.D.** ("Doctor of Jurisprudence," a law qualification).

dorm
a building providing living quarters for students at a school or college.

electives
the classes that high school or college students can choose to take depending on their interests or abilities. In high school these can include subjects such as foreign languages, home economics, computer science, car repair, and woodworking.

elementary school
the first formal school attended by American children. It usually follows **kindergarten** and covers from first grade to fifth or sixth grade, depending on the school system. It's also called **grade school.**

exchange student
a United States student who studies for a few months or a year in another country, while a student from the other country studies in the U.S. The visiting student is also called an exchange student.

extracurricular activities
anything a student does that is connected with the school but not related to course work, such as sports, music, or drama.

faculty
the members of the teaching staff at a college or university.

fees
the money that students must pay for things other than **tuition,** such as living expenses.

final (exam)
a test taken at the end of an academic term, when students are tested on all the material covered in a course. A student's grade on a final can count for as much as 50 percent of their total grade for a course.

financial aid
economic assistance in the form of scholarships, grants, student loans, etc., for students in schools and colleges.

floor
each floor of a dorm is a way of organizing the students who live there. Students on an individual floor often agree on their own

rules for visiting hours that may be stricter than the dorm's rules, and each floor usually has its own **RA.**

flunk

a slang term meaning to not pass a test or course; to fail. To flunk out of school or college is to have to leave the school and not finish one's course because of poor grades.

fraternity

a traditionally all-male social organization for college students. Its name is usually a combination of Greek letters.

freshman

a student in the first year of high school (ninth grade) or a four-year college.

grade school

another name for **elementary school.**

graduate school

the period of study for an advanced degree after a student has earned a four-year undergraduate degree. It's also called **grad school,** and can refer to the part of the university itself that offers graduate degrees.

graduate student

a general term for any student who is studying for a degree higher than a bachelor's degree.

graduation

the ceremony that marks the end of a person's high school or college career. Diplomas are handed out, and awards are given to students with special achievements.

grant

money given to a student to pay for college fees and tuition. Grants are given either to students with very little money or for work in a specific field or institution, and do not have to be repaid.

GRE

Graduate Record Examination; the standardized test taken by college graduates who want to go to graduate school. It tests math, verbal, and analytical skills.

Greek

a member of a college **fraternity** or **sorority.**

guidance counselor
⇨ **counselor**

gym
another word for **PE** class; also, the building where this class takes place. Gyms are also used for school assemblies, dances, and parties.

high school
the school attended by students between ninth or tenth and twelfth grades (between fourteen and eighteen years of age), where students get their secondary education. Students who complete the required coursework with passing grades receive a high school **diploma.**

homecoming
the season of activities that takes place at high schools, colleges, and universities, when graduates of the school come back to visit. It usually centers around a sports game (usually football) and a dance, and takes place sometime in the fall.

home economics
the school subject that covers topics such as cooking, nutrition, and hygiene, and also may cover other related topics, such as child development, family relationships, and consumer information. It is usually taken as an elective.

homeroom
the class that high school students go to first thing in the morning, where attendance is taken and students are given any general information that they may need about school events, activities, rules, etc.

honor roll
a list of the students with the best grades in a high school, usually announced every semester or quarter.

honor society
an organization that students with high grades at a school may be invited to join. There is also a national version of this, the National Honor Society or NHS. It is one of the achievements that is important to list on a college application.

instructor
the lowest rank for faculty in a college or university.

Ivy League
a group of eight old and prestigious colleges in the Northeast of the United States: Brown, Columbia, Cornell, Dartmouth, Harvard, Princeton, the University of Pennsylvania, and Yale.

jock
a slang term for someone whose main interest in high school or college is sports.

junior
a student in the third year of high school (eleventh grade) or a four-year college.

junior high school
the school attended by students between seventh grade and eighth or ninth grade. There are more classes than in elementary school, and students start going from one classroom to another for different subjects rather than staying in just one classroom.

junior year abroad
a year (usually the third, or junior year) spent studying at a university in another country. Students who do this are often called **JYAs.**

j.v./junior varsity
a less skilled team that represents a school or college in sports competitions.

kindergarten
the level of schooling attended by children before they start elementary school. **Kindergarteners** are usually five years old.

law school
the graduate courses that a student takes to earn a law degree, or the part of a university that offers these courses.

letter
to earn the right to wear the school letter on a school jacket, by playing on a **varsity** sports team: "I lettered in basketball."

LSAT
Law School Admissions Test; the test taken by college graduates who want to go to law school once they have earned their bachelor's degree.

magnet school

a public school that offers special training that is not available in every school in the district. For example, a school may specialize in computer science or music, and students throughout the district can attend special classes there for part of the day. In some districts, magnet schools are exclusive, and students must compete to be full-time students there.

major

the main subject in which a college student specializes. It is also a verb: "I majored in history in college."

makeup (test)

a test taken by a student who has missed a test for some reason. Not all teachers will allow students to make up missed tests.

master's degree

the degree earned by students who complete at least a year of further study after getting a bachelor's degree; also called an **M.A.**

math

mathematics. (Not "*maths.*")

MCAT

Medical College Admissions Test; the test taken by college graduates who want to go to medical school once they have earned their bachelor's degree.

medical school

the graduate courses that a student takes to earn a medical degree, or the part of a university that offers these courses. It's also called "med school."

middle school

the school attended by students between fifth or sixth grade and eighth grade. It is much the same as **junior high school.**

midterm

a test taken about halfway through an academic quarter, in which students are tested on the material covered during that time. Midterm grades will often count for a large percentage of a student's total grade in a class.

minor

a secondary subject in which a college student may specialize. It is also a verb: "I majored in biology and minored in math."

No. 2 pencil

a type of pencil with a medium-soft lead, used for taking standardized tests and tests that will be scored automatically by a machine.

nursery school

another word for **preschool**.

parochial school

a private school owned by a religious organization.

P.E.

a school class in which students learn to play many different sports; *P.T.*

pep assembly/rally

an assembly in which the cheerleading squad leads the students in cheers to build excitement for the school's sports teams.

period

one of the units of class time that the school day in middle, junior, and high schools is divided into, usually fifty minutes. Different periods are referred to as first period, second period, etc. There are typically six or seven class periods in a school day.

Ph.D.

a Doctor of Philosophy; the highest degree given by a university. It requires a minimum of two to three years of further study after a master's degree, along with an original **dissertation** and written and oral examinations.

place out

to be exempted from taking a required college course while getting college credits for it, usually done by getting a good score on an **AP** test.

play hooky

a slightly old-fashioned term that means to not go to classes in order to do something more fun.

pledge

to join a **fraternity** or **sorority** and promise to obey its rules.

postgraduate/postdoctoral student
a student with a doctorate who is doing further research and study at a university. The most common areas of postgraduate study are science and medicine. They're often called **postgrads** or **postdocs.**

prep school
a private high school that prepares students for college. Some prep schools also include junior high school.

preschool
a school attended by children between three and four years of age, before they start kindergarten. It's also called **nursery school.**

principal
the main administrative official in a school; *head teacher.*

private school
a school that is paid for by **tuition,** rather than by the government.

professor
the highest rank in the faculty at a college or university. A department can have any number of professors; the term is not limited to the holder of a university chair. It's also called **full professor.**

prom
a formal dance held in the spring, considered one of the most important events in the high school social calendar.

PTA
the Parent Teacher Association; a volunteer organization of parents and teachers who work together to improve the quality of education and educational facilities. There is also a nationally organized PTA. It's also called the **PA** (Parents' Association).

RA
Resident Assistant; an older college student, often a graduate student, who lives in a college **dorm** and is there to help students with problems and to make sure that dorm rules are followed. There is usually one RA per **floor.**

recess

the period of time in a school day when young children are allowed to go outside to play or have their lunch.

registration

the period at the beginning of a college or university quarter or semester when students choose, enroll in, and pay for the courses they want to take.

remedial class

a class you must take if your skills in a particular subject, especially English or math, are not strong enough for you to take part in the normal classes.

review

to go over all the material that will be on an exam. A review session will often be led by the teacher who taught the course, and is meant to prepare students for the exam.

room and board

a room in college-owned housing, and meals provided in college facilities, paid for by students as additional fees.

rush

the period when college **fraternities** and **sororities** have a series of parties and other social events to allow potential members to decide which one they want to join, and to allow these societies to evaluate potential members.

salutatorian

the student with the second-highest academic standing in a graduating class, who gives the welcoming speech in the graduation ceremony.

SAT

Scholastic Assessment Test; one of the standardized college entrance tests that American students take before applying to college.

scholarship

money for college fees and tuition given to a student, usually on the basis of academic merit, artistic talent, family need, or athletic ability. Scholarships do not have to be paid back.

school
an educational institution at any level.

school district
a local unit in charge of public school administration for an area. It is run by a school board that can set course requirements and that hires principals and makes overall budget decisions.

senior
a student in the fourth and final year of high school (twelfth grade) or a four-year college.

skip school/skip class
to not attend school or a particular class, especially to do something that might be considered more fun than studying.

sophomore
a student in the second year of high school (tenth grade) or a four-year college.

sorority
a traditionally all-female social organization for college students. Its name is usually a combination of Greek letters.

student council
a high school student organization, made up of officers elected by the other students, who organize student activities and represent student interests in school meetings.

student loan
a loan taken out by a student to help pay college fees and tuition.

student union
a building on a college campus where students can socialize, study, eat, etc.

study hall
a period of the school day when a student does not have a class and can go to the library or another place in the building to do schoolwork.

substitute (teacher)
a teacher who fills in for one who is absent or sick.

tenure
permanent job status earned by a professor at a college or university. It is very difficult for a school to fire a professor with tenure.

term paper
a lengthy written assignment, requiring some research, on a topic related to a high school or college course subject.

thesis
a long research paper, often one hundred pages or more, that is usually one of the requirements for students to earn a **master's degree.**

tuition
the money paid to attend classes at a school or college; *fees.*

tutor
someone who helps students who are having problems in a particular subject in either high school or college. Tutors are often students in a higher grade or in graduate school. They are not faculty members.

undergraduate
a student in the process of completing a **bachelor's degree.**

unit
⇨ **credit.**

valedictorian
the student with the highest academic standing in a graduating class, who gives the farewell speech in the graduation ceremony.

varsity
the main team that represents a school or college in sports competitions. Each sport has a varsity team and a **junior varsity** team.

work-study
a program that pays for part of a student's salary in a job, to make the student more attractive to local employers. Many work-study jobs are on campus.

Chapter Nine
Housing

🔑 Key Confusables:

British:	**American:**
bath	= *bathtub*
bedsit	= *studio/bachelor/efficiency apartment*
cloakroom	= *guest bathroom/half bathroom*
council estate	= *housing project*
estate	= *(housing) development*
estate agent	= *real estate broker, Realtor*
flat	= *apartment*
garden	= *yard*
power point	= *outlet, socket*
property	= *real estate*
rubbish	= *garbage/trash*
semi-detached house	= *duplex*
survey	= *appraisal*
tap	= *faucet*
terrace house	= *row house/town house*
toilet	= *bathroom*
wardrobe	= *closet*

🔑 Key Americanisms:

Americans call any person they share living quarters with a **roommate,** even if they live in a house or apartment.

Americans don't refer to the room that contains the toilet as "the toilet." They always call it the **bathroom** (in a home), or the **restroom,** the **ladies' room,** or the **men's room** (in public places). The men's room is never called "the gents'." Americans always say "I need to go to the bathroom," not "I need to use the toilet."

Americans refer to the ground floor of a building as the **first floor.** Therefore, what you know as the first floor is the **second floor,** and so on.

🗝 Key Grammar:

Americans say:
He lives on my street.
Apartment for rent.
May I use the bathroom/ restroom?
Nancy set the table.
Patrick is doing the dishes.
I'll call you tomorrow/I'll give you a call.

Americans *do not* say:
He lives in my street.
Flat to let.
Can I use the toilet?
Nancy laid the table.
Patrick is doing the washing up.
I'll ring you tomorrow/I'll give you a ring.

🗝 Key Cultural Points:

Owning their own house on their own piece of land is very important to Americans, but they are very mobile and often move every few years. In cities, they tend to rent until later in life, and buy only when they are fairly settled or starting a family. Because there is so much more space in the U.S. for building, and land in most places is not very expensive, houses take up more land than they do in many other countries.

There are a few large, densely populated cities like New York where people pay very high prices for rather small living spaces, but this is not the usual situation.

• •

Space

One of the first things that strikes people when they arrive in the United States is the amount of space everywhere—the size and scale of things is one of the defining characteristics of the country. The vast amount of space affects the way Americans think about where and how they live. While the large size of American houses, cars, and appliances may seem wasteful to you, to Americans it is just normal. Everything is big because it can be.

Another thing to keep in mind is that the United States is a relatively young country, just a little over two hundred years old, so try not to laugh when you hear Americans refer to buildings built in the early years of the twentieth century as "old."

The All-American House

Although there are many different types of houses in the United States, with variations depending on area and income level, the typical American house is recognizable across the country. An average, middle-class American home in an average, middle-class neighborhood will be a mid-sized building on its own plot of land, with a front lawn that is neat and well tended. (Neighbors will often complain if someone's lawn is overgrown or untidy.)

There will be a driveway and a covered garage, often attached to the house, that can hold two cars. Sometimes there is just a **carport**, or a carport in front of a garage, which is a space with a roof over it but no walls. **Porches** are common, especially in areas where the weather is mild. The **backyard** will similarly have a well-kept lawn, and might feature a **patio** or **deck** area with a barbecue and a table and chairs.

Americans may have a garden—a place where flowers or vegetables are grown—in their yards, but they do not call the land around the house a garden.

The house itself usually has one or two stories. A popular style is the **ranch house**—a one-story house with a low roof and an **open-plan** design inside. However, there are many styles of houses, which often vary according to region, and as you drive down an American street you will notice that few of the houses look the same. They may have a similar basic style, but the façade and front **yard** of each house will be as individual as its owner.

It may seem that many houses are very new and not very well built, but newer houses are not really intended to last more than fifty years. However, older houses are becoming more popular, provided they are old enough to be considered charming, and are built well enough to be worth fixing up. It is unlikely that a family will live in a house forever, let alone that the children will continue to live in it once they are grown up.

Bedrooms and Bathrooms

Bedrooms tend to be fairly large, if only to fit the extra-large beds Americans are fond of. The most common sizes for beds are, from largest to smallest, **king-size, queen-size, full-size** (or **double**), and **twin-size.** Most bedrooms have built-in **closets. Walk-in closets** are not unusual, and are not just for movie stars and other glamorous types. Stand-alone wardrobes are rarely used. When they are used, they tend to be more decorative than a practical place for storing clothes. Smaller articles of clothing are also stored in **dressers, bureaus,** or **chests of drawers.**

*Your **wardrobe** refers to the clothes you own. The large piece of wooden furniture for storing clothes is usually called an **armoire**, but clothes are more likely to be kept in a **closet**.*

The average family home has three bedrooms, with the **master bedroom** having its own bathroom. There is another full bathroom for the occupants of the other bedrooms to share. Sometimes there will also be a **guest** or **half bath(room)** (just a toilet and sink), especially if the house is built on more than one floor. Real estate agents will call a bathroom that has a shower but no bathtub a **three-quarter bath(room),** but the family in the house will just call this a bathroom.

A guest bathroom is never referred to as a cloakroom; a cloakroom is the place where coats are left when people arrive somewhere, especially a restaurant or a theater.

*Americans don't like using the word "toilet," and only use it to refer to the toilet bowl itself. A bathtub can be called a **tub**, but not a bath. A bath is what you take when you get in the bathtub.*

Americans prefer showers to baths, so there isn't always a bathtub in the bathroom. If there is a tub, though, there will nearly always be a shower fixture above it, with the shower plumbed in the wall, rather than having a pump box attached to it. Sinks usually have plenty of **counter** space around them, with storage space in cabinets underneath. They usually have a single spigot, with individual or combined taps for hot and cold water. A **tap** is one of the two water controls, not the spigot, and the whole fixture is called a **faucet.** Individual hot and cold water faucets are found in bathrooms in older houses, but mixed taps are so common that Americans don't call them mixed taps.

Something that might come as a shock (no pun intended) is that not only are light switches often found inside bathrooms, but there are also electrical **outlets** for things like hair dryers and shavers.

Look, Ma—No Doors!

Another striking feature of American homes is the lack of doors between rooms. Shared areas tend to flow into each other, with the front door opening into a hall that is open to the living room, which in turn is separated from the kitchen by a **breakfast bar** or counter. Sometimes you will find a separate formal living room, but as American lifestyles have become increasingly informal, these have been replaced by the all-purpose family room. The dining area may be either part of the living area or an extension of the kitchen.

Most modern homes have central air conditioning and heating, which means that it is not necessary to keep rooms closed off to keep in the warm or cool air. Older properties may have window-mounted air-conditioning units and conventional radiators, and a lot of houses have ceiling fans.

Appliances and Electricity

Electric current in the United States is 110/120 volts, and appliances and electrical equipment use a two-pronged plug. Sometimes there is a third prong that acts as a **ground.** There are no on/off switches on electrical outlets to regulate the power—it is just on all the time.

Plugs are attached to appliances by a **cord** *rather than a lead. Appliances are not earthed, they're* **grounded**.

Keep in mind the different voltage if you bring in foreign appliances. While converters and transformers may be used, make sure that the appliances themselves have a dual-voltage switch for changing from 240 to 110. They must also be capable of running at 60 Hertz rather than the standard 50 Hertz.

Furthermore, European TVs and **VCR**s will not work in North America because the NTSC transmission standard, which broadcasts on 525 lines, is used rather than PAL, which broadcasts on 625 lines. Another little quirk is that all light bulbs in the United States are of the screw type, rather than bayonet fitting.

HOUSING

The highest number of appliances and electrical gadgets is usually found in the kitchen. American kitchens are well equipped with a variety of labor-saving devices. Most obvious, of course, is the massive refrigerator/freezer. These two items are almost always integrated into one unit with two doors. Separate under-the-counter refrigerators and freezers are rarely seen in the United States.

Refrigerators are usually stocked with a few weeks' worth of food, because people tend to shop far less frequently and they buy more groceries in one trip, especially since the advent of the enormous **warehouse/superstore**. (➩ *Sales and Discount Shopping* on page 172). Other appliances that are commonly found in the American kitchen are the microwave oven, dishwasher, blender, bread maker, food processor, and **garbage disposal**.

The appliance used for cooking is called a **stove** *or a* **range**, *not a cooker. Ovens usually have a* **broiler**, *not a grill, and the broiler is part of the oven compartment itself. A* **grill** *is the metal rack you use for cooking over an open fire, as in a barbecue.*

The washing machine and clothes dryer are not usually found in the kitchen. Instead, they will be placed in a small room off the kitchen (called a **utility room**) or maybe in the basement, if the house has one. As with all other American appliances, washers and dryers are very large, and they are always separate components, rather than combination washer/dryers.

Dryers are not known as "tumble dryers."

The controls may also look unfamiliar, as they do not rely on the series of symbols that are standard in most of the rest of the world. They use a much more basic system of hot/warm/cold and a dial to control the length of the wash cycle and the water level. The care labels in clothes will usually give instructions that match these, e.g., "Machine wash warm, gentle cycle." Americans don't know how to read the symbols on the labels of imported clothes.

Televisions Everywhere

Another, possibly unexpected, piece of equipment in the kitchen is likely to be a small TV set—perfect for catching up on the news while making dinner. In fact, there are probably at least two TVs in the house—one in the living area and another in the master bedroom. It is not unusual to find TVs in the other bedrooms, too. Size matters when it comes to television, too, and big-screen TVs are popular. Another item in most American homes is the **VCR** or videocassette recorder.

Americans always call these machines VCRs, not videos, and shows are taped, not videoed.

Telephone Service

Telephone service is complicated in the United States, although generally cheaper than in other countries. You can buy a phone anywhere, not just from a telephone service provider. We won't talk about **cellular phones** (mobile phones) in this chapter because they work the same as they do everywhere, except to say that the service is not international and may not reach all areas of the United States.

HOUSING

Your home or business telephone number will have seven digits. To call outside your local service area, you must dial a 1, then the three-digit **area code**, then the number. To call internationally, dial 011, then the country code, then the number. You have to drop the 0 from the regional code on British telephone numbers. Country codes are listed in telephone books, which are free to telephone customers and are usually hanging from public **phone booths**, unless someone has stolen them. Local calls from phone booths cost 25¢ or 35¢ no matter how long you talk.

Telephones have letters on the buttons as well as numbers. Many businesses have **800 or 888 numbers** *which are toll-free, and they like to use the letters as easier ways for customers to remember their number, as in 1-800-GET TOYS. (We have no idea if this is a real phone number or not—we made it up.)*

Local Telephone Service

The American telephone system can be confusing, because different companies provide local and long-distance telephone service. Until recently, you could not choose your local service provider, although this is changing. Local telephone service is still mostly provided by local phone companies owned by one of seven regional holding companies, or RHCs, which cover different areas of the country. The seven RHCs serve the following areas:

Ameritech—Illinois, Indiana, Michigan, Ohio, and Wisconsin
Bell Atlantic—Delaware, the District of Columbia, Maryland, New Jersey, Pennsylvania, Virginia, West Virginia, and New York
Bell South—Alabama, Florida, Georgia, Kentucky, Louisiana, Mississippi, the Carolinas, and Tennessee
Nynex—New England and some parts of New York
Pacific Telesis Group (or PacTel)—California and Nevada
Southwestern Bell Corporation—Arkansas, Kansas, Missouri, Oklahoma, and Texas
U.S. West—the remaining states except Hawaii and Alaska

There are many smaller companies that provide local phone service now, as well as one other national company, GTE Corporation (not an RHC), operating mostly in California, Florida, and Hawaii.

Internet Use

In many homes, there is likely to be a computer somewhere in the house. More and more Americans are comfortable with computers and the Internet, and make use of them on a daily basis. Internet connections typically go through local phone lines, and are usually paid for by monthly fees. With local calls free in many places, or with a generous call allowance as part of the monthly phone rates, home use of e-mail and the Internet is extremely common.

Long-distance Telephone Service

Long-distance service is provided by one of about five hundred **long-distance carriers.** The largest of these is the American Telephone and Telegraph Company (AT&T), with Sprint and MCI not far behind. Long distance is a fiercely competitive market, and it is best to shop around and ask the opinion of friends and colleagues before choosing a carrier. Local telephone service is regulated by state government agencies, while the Federal Communications Commission (FCC) is in charge of telephone service that crosses state lines.

In order to call someone, and have them pay for the call, callers should dial the operator and ask to make a **collect call***, or to* **call collect***. Do not ask the operator to reverse the charges. You can avoid the operator by calling 1-800-COLLECT.*

❗ **Warning:** *In recent years, a practice known as "slamming" has arisen, in which a person making a long-distance phone call is switched to another long-distance carrier without their knowledge, often at a higher cost. Slamming is illegal, and if it happens to you, you should report it to the police.*

Utilities

Services such as electricity, gas, water, and waste disposal are known as **utilities** in the United States. Most utilities are provided by private corporations, but they are closely regulated by state and local government authorities in order to protect the public. They set service and safety standards, as well as establishing rates and charges for each utility.

Some companies provide more than one service, so they may send a combined bill for electricity and gas, for example. Utilities must be in the name of the person who lives in a house or apartment, and a returnable deposit of $50 to $300 may be required before a service is provided. There may also be a connection fee. Water rates may be charged separately, or they may be included in local property taxes.

Garbage Collection

Garbage collection fees may also be included in property taxes, or billed separately. Garbage collection is usually organized by city authorities, but it may be done by a private company. It is picked up in **garbage trucks** by **garbage collectors** or **sanitation workers.** People who live in houses have to put their garbage out in large **garbage cans** on specific days and times (usually twice a week).

In apartment buildings or complexes, there are large bins or **Dumpsters** (a trademarked name for a skip) in which residents can place their bagged garbage. Sometimes there is a chute with openings on each floor for placing the garbage in, which is then collected in the basement of the building.

*Americans don't use the word "rubbish." They will sometimes refer to an idea that they think is stupid as **garbage**, but not as often as British speakers use "rubbish." They use a lot of words that are not polite instead, such as "bull," "bullshit," "bunk," "malarkey," and "crap." The more polite thing to say is "That's ridiculous."*

HOUSING

Recycling

Most cities now require some form of recycling. Residents separate their paper trash into one container, bottles and cans into another, and other garbage into regular garbage cans. Your recycling is put out with the garbage for collection once a week. Some cities charge a fine if you put recyclable items in the garbage. We'd rather not think about the poor person whose job it is to find out if you are breaking this law.

Housing Options

Of course, not all Americans live in a detached single-family house. In large cities, for example, many people live in **apartments.** These are usually found in apartment buildings, with a few apartments on each floor of a relatively tall building, although large older houses are also divided into apartments.

In smaller cities, where there is more space for building horizontally, **apartment complexes** are a common sight—large developments of two- and three-story buildings containing a variety of different-sized apartments. They have facilities such as laundry rooms, swimming pools, and gyms for the use of the residents. A management company usually owns and runs these complexes.

A quirk of American buildings is that there is hardly ever a thirteenth floor in them because it is considered bad luck. The numbering of the floors skips from the twelfth to the fourteenth.

Most people who live in apartments rent them, but there are a few options for people who want to own their apartments. The first and probably most common is the **condominium** or **condo.** The apartment is owned by the person who lives in it, who pays a **maintenance fee** for the upkeep of the building and for the use of any facilities in the building. Another option is the **co-op,** in which the owners form a corporation to own and manage a building and then buy shares in the corporation that entitles them to live in it.

Choosy Neighbors

Ever since suburbs were developed, Americans have liked to choose the sort of community or neighborhood their house is in. Those looking for a house can choose exactly the type of neighborhood that best suits them, from ordinary residential areas to exclusive developments around a **country club.**

Some of the newer types of residential areas are **gated communities** and **planned communities.** A gated community is a development in which there is a barrier at the entrance with either a security guard or an electronic security device that watches who goes in and out to create a safer environment. A planned community is a development that may include areas planned for parks, schools, and stores. House owners are usually required to sign a **covenant** with rules about external decorations, building restrictions, and use of the property. Obviously, this is a bit too strict for some people.

Not everybody in the United States is rich enough to have quite so many housing options available to them. In urban areas, **housing projects,** or simply **the projects,** are home to the poorer members of society. The rent for apartments in housing projects is controlled so that it does not rise too quickly.

In smaller cities and rural areas, **trailers,** or **mobile homes,** are available to buy or rent. Although they are all rectangular in shape and are not very solid, they can look very much like small houses when they are finished. Trailers are parked in a **trailer park,** where they can be hooked up to services and utilities.

Buying a Home

About two-thirds of all Americans own their homes. Once the decision has been made to buy a house, and a neighborhood or development selected, the first stop for potential buyers is a **Realtor,** or a **real estate agent** or **broker.** All real estate agents and brokers must be licensed by the state they want to practice in after completing courses and passing a test on the subject.

Realtor *is a registered name for a real estate agent who is a member of the National Association of Realtors, and members have to follow the Association's Code of Ethics. Their offices can be called a* **Realty**.

Real estate brokers do not always display pictures of properties for sale in their windows. Rather, buyers make an appointment to see a broker, who will then show them any properties in their chosen area and price range.

Mortgages are arranged through banks, **savings and loan associations**, mortgage or insurance companies, and other financial institutions. A **down payment** of about 10 percent of the purchase price is required. This money should be held in an **escrow** account until the deal is closed. The lender will require an **appraisal** of the property before authorizing a loan, and will also require proof that enough mortgage insurance is bought once the property is sold.

Renting

Many Americans will rent a house or apartment for years without thinking about buying a home. This is partly because renting is usually cheaper than buying, but also because they tend to move around a lot more, so it does not make sense to tie themselves down by owning a house. In places like New York City and San Francisco, however, rents are incredibly high, due to the high demand for living space in an already crowded place.

While there is no guaranteed standard for rental properties, good, spacious accommodation is available across the country. In some places, where rental properties are easier to find, renting an apartment is pretty simple, although renters may be asked for personal and job references, and banking and credit histories. If the apartment is particularly desirable, there may be a large number of other applicants, so the landlord can choose the tenant with the best references.

A **security deposit** of one month's rent is usually necessary, and tenants must typically sign a lease for a term of one year. Landlords prefer not to rent to any tenants who are paying more than a quarter or a third of their monthly income on rent. You may also lose your deposit if you break the lease by leaving a place before the lease is ended.

Glossary of American Terms

apartment
a living unit in either a building or an apartment complex.

apartment complex
a group of similar buildings containing a variety of different-sized apartments and managed by one company. Apartment complexes often include facilities such as laundry rooms, tennis courts, and swimming pools.

area code
a three-digit number that represents a particular telephone service area.

appraisal
an evaluation that is done to determine the value of a property and whether it can be approved for a mortgage.

armoire
a large piece of wooden furniture used for storing clothes; *wardrobe*.

backyard
the area at the back of a house, usually with a lawn, and sometimes a patio or deck.

bathroom
any room containing a toilet. It is called a bathroom regardless of the presence of bathing facilities.

breakfast bar
a bar or counter in a kitchen used for informal meals. It usually connects a kitchen with the family or living room beyond it.

brownstone
a type of building common in the Northeast of the country, usu-ally a tall, narrow **row house** faced with a reddish-brown sand-stone. Many brownstones are divided into apartments.

builder
a contractor, or someone who develops, builds, and sells houses or apartments.

bureau
another word for a **dresser.**

burner
the part of a **range** where you place a pan to cook over a flame (on a gas stove) or on a hot metal ring (on an electric stove).

carport
a space next to a house for a car to be parked in, that has a roof but has posts instead of walls.

cellular phone, cell phone
a mobile phone.

chest of drawers
another word for a **dresser.**

closet
a place in a room for storing clothes and other objects. Closets are usually built-in—built into an alcove or small room when the house is built.

collateral
something that you own, usually a house, that you offer as a guarantee against a loan. If you do not pay back the loan, the institution that gave you the loan can force you to sell your col-lateral to pay the loan back.

condominium, condo
an apartment building or complex in which the individual units are owned by the people who live in them, or one of these apart-ments.

contractor
a person with whom you contract to build something or carry out some work on your house, who is then responsible for getting the materials and supervising the work.

co-op, cooperative

a corporation that is formed to plan, finance, build, and manage an apartment building or complex. Individuals buy shares in the corporation that allow them to live in the housing units, but not to own them. All residents contribute toward maintenance, repairs, and any improvements made to the building.

cord

the flexible, electric cable with a plug at the end for connecting an appliance to the power source; *lead*.

counter

a flat surface around sinks and along walls in kitchens and bathrooms; *worktop*.

country club

a club that offers its members facilities such as a golf course, tennis courts, and swimming pools, as well as a restaurant and clubhouse, and often built at the heart of a residential **development**.

covenant

an agreement that someone signs in order to buy or build a house in a planned community, in which they agree to rules about property use, building restrictions, etc.

deck

a raised wooden platform at the back of a house, which is often used for eating outdoors. Compare **porch**.

den

a large, comfortable, casual room for family activities such as watching TV, playing games, or just hanging out. Dens are sometimes built in basements and are known for having wood paneling on the walls; also called a **family room**.

development, housing development

a group of similar individual houses that are built and sold by a management company; *estate*.

doorman

in some city apartments, a uniformed attendant at the door of the building.

double bed

another word for **full-size**.

down payment
an amount of money that is paid as part of the purchase price of something like a house or vehicle, with the balance of the price to be repaid later.

dresser
a piece of furniture with drawers in it used for storing clothes; also called a **bureau** or a **chest of drawers.**

driveway
a paved area leading from a street to a house's garage or **carport.**

Dumpster
a large metal container for the disposal of garbage that can then be easily emptied into a garbage truck; *skip.*

duplex
a building that contains two houses, with one shared side wall; *semi-detached house.*

duplex apartment
an apartment built over two floors.

800 number/888 number
a telephone number of a business that is free of charge for customers; *freefone number.*

escrow
an amount of money, a deed, or a piece of property that is held as security until the purchase of a house is complete.

family room
another word for a **den.**

faucet
the sink fixture that includes the spigot (the part that the water comes out of) and one or two **taps.**

fixer-upper
a house or other property that is sold at a very low price because it needs a lot of repairs and improvements.

full-size
the size of bed between queen-size and twin-size; 54" × 75"; also called a **double bed.**

HOUSING

garbage

the American word for *rubbish*. Garbage usually contains wet rubbish as well as dry.

garbage can

a large receptacle for disposing of waste material.

garbage disposal

an electric device that gets rid of organic waste such as vegetable peelings by grinding it and flushing it down the kitchen sink.

garbage truck

a large vehicle used for the collection of waste material.

gated community

a residential development with gates and security guards for the increased security of the residents.

ground

to connect a piece of electrical equipment to the ground in order to make it safer; to *earth* something.

home improvement

any work done to make a house or apartment more comfortable, attractive, or valuable. Americans do not say *DIY*, although they do sometimes talk about do-it-yourself projects.

home improvement loan

a loan made by a financial institution, usually with a person's house as **collateral**, for making repairs or improvements to that house.

king-size

the largest size bed; 76" × 80".

laundry room

a room in a house for the washing machine and dryer and everything else to do with laundry. In an apartment building or complex, it's a room containing coin-operated washing machines and dryers for the use of the residents.

long-distance carrier

a company that provides long-distance telephone services.

maintenance

the things that someone does to make sure that a building is kept clean and in good condition.

master bedroom
the main or largest bedroom in a house or apartment.

mobile home
a small house with a steel frame meant to be moved on wheels to its permanent location.

nightstand
a small table placed by the side of a bed; *bedside table.*

open-plan
a design for a house in which one room leads to another without doors, or even walls, between them.

outlet
the point in a wall or floor where an electrical appliance is plugged in; *power point.*

patio
a paved area outside of a house, which is often used for eating outdoors.

phone booth
a public shelter with a phone in it; *phone box.*

planned community
a housing development that is planned to include residential areas, schools, parks, and stores.

porch
a raised, covered platform that often forms the entrance to a house. They can also be found on the sides or at the back of a house. A porch will often have chairs or a large swing for people to sit on.

(housing) project
a building or group of buildings built through government funding to provide housing for lower-income families.

queen-size
the size of bed between king-size and full-size; 60" × 80".

ranch house
a popular style of house, on a single level, with a low roof and an open-plan design.

range
the top of a stove that has **burners** on it; *cooker*. It's also another word for a **stove**.

rent control
laws set by the government (state or local) establishing how much rent landlords can demand, and how much it can increase year by year.

rent-stabilized
Tenants in rent-stabilized properties are protected by laws that control how much rent can be increased when renewing a lease.

retirement community
a housing development for older people, where they can often live independently but still have ready access to medical and other assistance if necessary.

roommate
someone with whom you share a room, apartment, or house.

row house
house in a series of houses that share side walls. They're common in the North and East of the country; *terraced house*. In the West, they are often called **town houses.**

savings and loan association
a financial institution that provides savings accounts and invests mostly in home mortgages; *building society*.

security deposit
the amount of money that must be paid in order to rent a property, which is usually returned when you leave the property. The deposit covers any damages to the property. Most landlords will not allow you to use the security deposit as your last month's rent.

shotgun house
a long, narrow house, with all the rooms off one corridor that runs the length of the house. These are most commonly found in the South. The name comes because a gun could be fired at one end and the bullet could exit at the other door.

socket
the point in a wall or floor where an electrical appliance is plugged in.

HOUSING

stoop
a set of steps leading up to the door of a house or building, usually big enough to sit on.

stove
an appliance that uses gas or electricity for cooking food. It usually has four **burners** on top and an oven underneath.

subdivision
an area of land used for building houses, usually by a developer or builder.

sublet
to rent a property from the person who rents it, especially for a limited time.

super, superintendent
the person in charge of **maintenance** in an apartment building.

tap
one of the controls for hot and cold water on a **faucet.** Many American faucets have only one control.

toilet
the ceramic fixture itself. "Toilet" is not used for the room in which it is located.

town house
one in a row of houses that share side walls.

trailer
a large, furnished van without a motor that can be used as a home when parked in a **trailer park.**

trailer park
a place where people can rent space to park their trailers and are provided with utilities and other services.

trash
another word for **garbage.** Some people use "trash" for dry *rubbish* such as paper, and "garbage" for wet rubbish.

twin-size
the smallest size bed; 39" × 75".

utilities
services such as water, gas, and electricity.

utility room

a small room in a house with a washer and dryer in it, often with shelves or cabinets and room for an ironing board; also called a **laundry room.**

VCR

videocassette recorder; a piece of electronic equipment used for playing and recording movies and TV shows on videotape.

Victorian

a type of house built late in the nineteenth century. They are large wooden structures with elaborate decorative and architectural features.

walk-in closet

a large closet, usually with hanging space on two or more sides.

walk-up

an apartment in a building without an elevator.

wardrobe

the clothes that you own: *She has a nice wardrobe* means "She wears nice clothes." ⇨ *armoire.*

yard

the land around a house, often with a lawn and flower beds.

Chapter Ten
Everyday Life

🔑 Key Confusables:

British	American
bookshop	= *bookstore*
cash till/cashpoint	= *ATM*
chemist's	= *drugstore/pharmacy*
cheque	= *check*
corner shop	= *convenience store*
current account	= *checking account*
deposit account	= *savings account*
grocer's	= *grocery (store)*
jumper	= *sweater*
newsagent	= *newsstand*
note	= *bill*
off-licence	= *liquor store/package store*
pants	= *underpants/panties/shorts*
pay in	= *deposit*
post	= *mail*
queue	= *line up/wait in line*
shop assistant	= *salesperson/sales assistant*
shopping centre	= *(shopping) mall*
till	= *cash register/checkout*
trolley	= *cart*
trousers	= *pants*
zip	= *zipper*

🔑 Key Americanism:

The word "store" is used to talk about most places where you buy things. "Shop" is usually used for smaller stores that specialize in a particular type of product.

⊶ Key Grammar:

Americans say:
I'm going to the grocery (store).
He's getting the groceries.
Have you deposited that check?
Can you mail this letter for me?
Can I help you?

Americans *do not* say:
I'm going shopping.
He's doing the shopping.
Have you paid in that cheque?
Can you post this letter for me?
Are you being served?

⊶ Key Cultural Points:

Americans are some of the biggest consumers in the world, and stores provide a vast amount of choice.

Although most Americans can pay full price for things, they love bargains, sales, and discount shopping.

• •

The Basics

This chapter deals with all the basic activities—shopping, banking, mail—that someone living in the United States would have to deal with on a daily basis.

Money

The basic unit of American currency is the dollar **bill.** The other denominations available are five, ten, twenty, fifty, and one hundred dollars. There are a number of slang terms for the various bills, the most common one being **buck.**

American paper money is never referred to as "notes."

When saying a price out loud, people usually don't say "dollar" in the amount. So $12.99 would be "twelve ninety-nine," and not "twelve dollars ninety-nine." If they say the full amount, it's "twelve dollars and ninety-nine cents."

EVERYDAY LIFE

Banking

Most American banks are not part of national chains. They are most likely owned and operated on a regional or state basis, although a few big banks are present across the country. A current account, or one that allows clients to write checks and withdraw money through **ATMs,** is known as a **checking account.** A deposit account is called a **savings account.** Banks offer a variety of accounts with different conditions and rates of interest.

Checks

Americans use **checks** (cheques) frequently, but it is important to remember that most businesses will not accept checks from another state. Checks are printed with the account holder's name, address, and telephone number, and two forms of ID are usually required when paying by check—most likely a state driver's license and a major credit card. Banks do not issue check guarantee cards. In addition, bank clients must pay for checks, which are usually ordered in boxes of about two hundred checks for approximately $10 to $15.

Bank clients should avoid being overdrawn at all costs, as it can be damaging to their credit rating and they will have to pay heavy fines, both to the bank and to the business where the check was written. Deliberately writing a bad check is considered a crime in many places. It's known informally as **bouncing** a check. People do not arrange overdraft limits in advance.

ATMs

ATM stands for "automated-teller machine," a machine from which you can take money out of your checking account. ATMs are located not just outside banks, but in neighborhood stores and shopping malls. The word "ATM" is so common that you will see signs in store windows that say "ATM Machine Inside" although that's redundant. Some ATMs charge a fee of $1 to $2. The secret number you key in to use the machine is called a **PIN**

number, which is also redundant because PIN means "personal identification number."

Debit Cards

Debit cards are becoming more and more common in the United States, especially because you need no other form of ID to use them. Many ATM cards double as debit cards. Some places will have you sign the receipt as if you had paid with a charge card, and others will ask you to key in your PIN on a special keypad. Some cards can be debit or credit cards, depending on what you want, so clerks will usually ask you "debit or credit?" when you hand them your card. You can also ask for cash back from many stores when you use your debit card to buy things, which is a way to avoid ATM fees.

Debit cards are not called check cards (and certainly not cheque cards, which as you now know do not exist in the United States).

Wiring Money

You can send money internationally using a wire service such as Western Union. They charge a percentage of the amount of money you send. Banks also wire money, but you have to have an account with them.

Traveler's Checks

You can usually use a traveler's check to buy things or pay for meals in restaurants, and you will get your change in U.S. currency. You don't have to go to a bank to cash it first. However, stores and restaurants will not cash your check if you don't buy something from them. Smaller places may not accept traveler's checks, so it's best to ask first.

The U.S. Postal Service

In terms of vocabulary, this tends to be a rather tricky category. The official service is known as the U.S. Postal Service, yet what it does is regulate and deliver **mail,** not the post. The place where people go to purchase stamps (also called postage stamps) and to send letters and packages is the post office, but the place you put your letters in is called a **mailbox,** not a post box.

Post offices do not act as banks, but you can buy **money orders** there if you don't have a checking account, and they have tax forms and passport applications. You also cannot make long-distance telephone calls from a post office.

There are four classes of mail in the United States. First class is for sending letters and postcards; second class is for magazines and newspapers; third class is for sending books and circulars; and fourth class includes everything else. Mail that needs to arrive overnight should be sent by **express mail.** Mail can also be sent **special delivery** for an additional charge, and it will be delivered by messenger rather than by a regular delivery.

The term **mailman** is more commonly used than postman, although in these days of heightened awareness of sexist language, the term **mail carrier** is preferred.

Stamps are sold at post offices and from vending machines and can sometimes be bought in supermarkets and drugstores.

Sending and Receiving Letters and Packages

The post office wants people to put their own address, called the **return address,** on the upper-left-hand corner of an envelope or package, rather than inside on the letter itself. If for some reason your letter or package cannot be delivered, it will be returned to you if your address is on the outside.

Addresses in the United States use a two-letter abbreviation for the state and a **ZIP code** after the state. The ZIP code is a five-digit number that helps a local post office find your address more accurately. In 1983, an additional four-digit code was added to ZIP codes that included further delivery information, but most people continue to use just the five-digit number.

Letters can be put in blue mailboxes found on city streets, or they can be put in a home's own mailbox where mail is delivered. The mail carrier will pick them up when delivering the day's mail. Private mailboxes often have a little red flag that can be raised to show that mail is waiting to be picked up.

Mailboxes are usually found by the sidewalk at the edge of a house's property, rather than mail being dropped through a slot in the door. Some houses, especially in cities, have a metal box attached to the house near the front door. In apartment buildings, mail will be put in individual boxes just inside the door; mail carriers do not usually pick up outgoing mail from apartment buildings.

Packages that weigh more than one pound have to be taken to the post office to be mailed. Packages are cheaper to send than letters as long as you don't put a letter inside the package; if you do, and you are silly enough to tell them you have, you will be charged the full letter rate for the weight of the package.

Post Office Boxes

You can rent a post office box to receive your mail at a post office instead of at home. People do this for many reasons: they might own a business and choose to keep the business mail separate from their personal mail, or they might move a lot within an area and want to keep a steady address. Post office boxes are not usually acceptable as addresses for your driver's license or to credit card companies.

Special Mail Companies

Letters and packages take anywhere from one to seven days to arrive by regular mail. If you want to send a letter or package faster, you can use the Post Office's Express Mail service, which is cheapest, or you can use one of the private companies that specialize in overnight deliveries. The biggest ones are Federal Express, United Parcel Service (UPS), and DHL. You have to use these companies' labels, which you can get just by telephoning them or going to a store such as Mail Boxes, Etc. that offers mailing services separately from the Post Office.

Laundry and Dry Cleaning

Most towns and cities have **Laundromats,** businesses that provide coin-operated washing machines and dryers. It is best to collect the necessary quarters before going, because coin-changing facilities may not always be available. Customers can sometimes pay an additional fee to have their laundry done by an attendant. Some Laundromats provide TVs, video games, and vending machines for customers.

Dry cleaners are also readily available, although, as with dry cleaners everywhere, the service is expensive. Many dry cleaners also offer a laundry and ironing service for shirts.

Where to Shop for What

The United States is the land of consumer choice, but it is helpful to know where to actually look for particular things, since the American names for many stores can be different, and some products are sold in unexpected places. An ironic example of this is that cigarettes are sold in **drugstores** in the United States, alongside the nicotine patches and gum.

A big difference to keep in mind is that Americans do not refer to stores using the possessive form of whatever product or service is offered there. So terms like "chemist's," "newsagent's," and "grocer's" are not used. Instead, the full name of the place is used: drugstore, **newsstand,** or **grocery store.** Do not add the possessive "s" if using a store's proper name unless there is actually a possessive in it, as in Bloomingdale's or Macy's, but not in Barnes & Noble or Safeway.

In general, Americans shop for food and other household products at large **groceries** or supermarkets. The convenience of one-stop shopping has almost done away with small, individually owned specialist shops. These days, supermarkets carry more than just food. Besides health and beauty aids and cleaning products, supermarkets often have in-store bakeries and delis selling prepared food, as well as pharmacies, film developing counters, and video rental facilities. Why go anywhere else?

Words like "fishmonger" and "greengrocer" are not used in American English, mainly because there are few of these shops around.

Fresh fruit and vegetables are called **produce**, *and they are sold in the produce section of a grocery store or at a* **produce stand**.

Alcoholic beverages are sold in supermarkets, **convenience stores,** and **liquor stores** or **package stores.** Most states regulate the hours during which alcohol, particularly hard liquor, may be purchased. Sometimes city and county regulations also apply. In some parts of the country, **blue laws** may apply, which regulate Sunday business activities. (⇨ *Shopping for Food and Drinks* on page 35.)

Cigarettes, can be bought in supermarkets, convenience stores, drugstores, and from vending machines in some restaurants and bars. The legal age for buying tobacco products is eighteen.

For products for home repairs and decorating, Americans head for **hardware stores** or **home improvement** stores, which stock most everything from power tools to wallpaper, and everything in between.

Newspapers and magazines are sold in a number of places: convenience stores, supermarkets, bookstores, and **newsstands.** Newsstands are small kiosks on sidewalks and in train stations that sell newspapers, magazines, and candy, and are more common in larger cities where people actually do some walking.

Housewares, appliances, and furniture are available in large stores dedicated to these items, and in **department stores.** Housewares and some furniture are also sold at the large discount retailers that have grown around the country in recent years.

Clothes and shoes are also sold in a variety of places, although most clothing stores are located in **malls.** Malls have large department stores that carry clothes for men, women, and children, as well as specialty stores that offer a particular type of clothing, or clothing for a specific group, such as children, teenagers, men, women, or **plus size** customers.

Department Stores

Department stores were the original places where you could buy everything you wanted under one roof. They now have a lot of competition from discount stores, so they keep their customers by offering special services and more high-quality items than can be found in discount stores. Department stores will let you return an item for whatever reason—it didn't fit, it wore out too quickly, or you just didn't like it.

These stores usually have nice facilities for customers, including a restaurant, clean bathrooms, and fitting rooms. In many of them, the sales assistants will ask you if you need help finding anything, and "start" a fitting room for you. This means that they take the clothes you are gathering to a fitting room so that you don't have to carry them around with you while choosing more clothes to try on. There is often no limit to the number of clothes you can bring into a fitting room to try on.

Sales and Discount Shopping

Most people love a bargain, and a whole industry has developed in the United States to offer American shoppers the best prices on most products. Most department stores and specialty stores have sales throughout the year and big end-of-season sales twice a year, where very good bargains can be found. However, there are a number of stores that offer lower prices year-round.

Discount Retailers

Discount retailers, or **mass merchandisers**, have appeared around the country relatively recently. These stores offer lower prices on everything from food, clothes, and toys to CDs, electronic equipment, and tools, by operating huge, **no-frills** stores, usually in suburban locations. They carry all the major brands, as well as some **store brands**, and since they buy in mass amounts, they are able to pass the savings on to customers.

Factory Outlets

Outlet shopping is another good option for finding quality goods at bargain prices. These are stores that carry **brand name** merchandise of all sorts (clothes, sporting goods, luggage, housewares) and are able to sell it at very low prices because the articles are no longer being made by the manufacturers, or because they are **seconds** (products that have slight flaws in them). Most of the defects are not apparent to most people. Outlets are also a way for famous designers to sell clothes when they have made too many in a particular season, so you can get some very high-quality things at these stores.

Warehouse Clubs

Another type of store that has changed American shopping is the **warehouse club.** These are very large stores housed in, as the name implies, warehouses, which offer their products **in bulk.** They charge customers a yearly fee of about $30. In turn, members save much more than that, usually on their first shopping trip. Warehouse clubs sell mostly household and grocery items, although they often don't carry fresh produce. They also have things like office equipment, casual wear, toys, and sporting goods.

Mail Order Shopping

Shoppers in the United States have long enjoyed the convenience of **mail order** shopping, ordering products either from **catalogs,** or from places that advertise on TV in **commercials** or **infomercials.** While it is still referred to as mail order, most

EVERYDAY LIFE

products are ordered over the phone (many companies have free 1-800 numbers) rather than through the mail.

Mail order companies either specialize in selling their own products, such as outdoor clothing and equipment, or will gather together a selection of products from different manufacturers aimed at a particular type of buyer, such as a business traveler. Some stores also have a mail order department; in fact, companies like Sears started out as mail order firms. Other stores put together a Christmas catalog, with gift suggestions, along with special products that are available only for the holidays.

In recent years, many mail order companies have gone online and started selling their products over the Internet. In addition, many companies have sprung up that exist only electronically. These companies are often able to offer merchandise at a discount, because they don't have to pay the **overhead** that traditional store owners deal with. However, by the time sales tax and **shipping and handling** are added in, the product may not be as cheap as it first seemed. But customers still get the convenience of shopping from home, as well as having access to products that perhaps are not available in their area.

A further twist on electronic shopping is the **e-auction**, which allows potential buyers to bid on merchandise of all kinds. The person who placed the highest bid by the end of the limited bidding period gets to buy the item.

Taxes

Although shopping in the United States may be considerably less expensive than in other countries, it may come as something of a shock when purchases are totaled, and the total is a lot more than what it said on the price tag. This is because sales tax is not included in the price displayed on the tag; it is added only at the time of purchase.

The amount of sales tax charged varies from state to state, although it averages around 8 percent. In some places, people who are not residents of the United States may claim back the tax they have paid on their purchases. A few states do not have sales tax.

Clothes

The subject of clothes is one area in which British and American English vary tremendously. There are several instances where the same word is used for completely different things, and just as many that have completely different names. There is also a category of words, such as *trousers*, that were in common usage in the United States as recently as forty years ago but are now considered slightly old-fashioned, although most people would understand the word. The following is a list of direct equivalents:

British	American
anorak	*parka*
Babygro™	*sleeper*
balaclava	*ski mask*
bathing costume	*swimsuit, bathing suit*
body	*leotard*
boiler suit	*coveralls*
bowler (hat)	*derby*
braces	*suspenders*
brogues	*oxfords*
bum bag	*fanny pack*
court shoes	*pumps*
cravat	*ascot*
diamanté	*rhinestone*
dinner jacket	*tuxedo*
dummy (for baby)	*pacifier*
dungarees	*overalls*
flies	*fly (on pants)*
handbag	*purse*
jim-jams	*jammies, p.j.'s, pajamas*
jumper	*sweater*

(continued)

British	**American**
knickers	*panties (knickers, or knickerbockers, are old-fashioned plus-fours)*
lounge suit	*business suit*
mac	*raincoat*
nappy	*diaper*
nightdress	*nightgown*
pants	*underpants; panties (women); shorts/briefs (men)*
pinafore	*jumper*
plimsolls	*canvas sneakers, slip-ons*
polo neck	*turtleneck*
popper	*snap (fastener)*
pumps	*canvas sneakers*
spectacles	*glasses*
sports jacket	*sports coat/blazer*
suspenders	*garter belt*
tights	*pantyhose (unless thick, opaque type)*
tracksuit	*sweats/sweatpants/sweatshirt*
trainers	*sneakers/tennis shoes/athletic shoes*
trousers	*pants*
turn-ups	*cuffs*
turtle neck	*mock turtleneck*
vest	*undershirt*
waistcoat	*vest*
Wellies	*rubber boots*
Y-fronts	*Jockey shorts, briefs*
zip	*zipper*

EVERYDAY LIFE

Around the House

There are also many vocabulary differences when it comes to housewares and products that are used around the house for cleaning and maintenance. Here is another list of British English terms and their American equivalents:

British	American
aluminium foil	aluminum foil
blind	(window) shade
camp bed	cot
carrycot	baby carrier/portacrib
Clingfilm	saran wrap/plastic wrap
clothespeg	clothespin
cot	crib
cotton reel	spool of thread
crack filler	Spackle™
crib	bassinet
curtains	drapes, curtains
dresser	hutch (a dresser is a chest of drawers)
duvet	comforter
emulsion paint	latex paint
flannel	washcloth
footstool	ottoman
hessian	burlap
Hoover™	vacuum cleaner
hosepipe	hose
loo roll	toilet paper, TP; some packages call it bathroom tissue
net curtains	sheers
pelmet	valance
plaster	Band-Aid™
pram	baby carriage
pushchair	stroller
rug (light blanket)	throw
secateurs	pruning shears
serviette	napkin
settee	couch/sofa/davenport
sideboard	buffet
skirting board	baseboard
spanner	wrench

(continued)

British	**American**
tea towel	*dishtowel*
truckle bed	*trundle bed*
valance	*dust ruffle*
washing powder	*laundry detergent*
washing-up liquid	*dishwashing liquid*

....

Glossary of American Terms

ATM
automated-teller machine; a machine located in the outside wall of a bank and inside some stores that allows bank customers to take out money and do other transactions.

bill
a piece of paper money; *note*.

blue law
a law that regulates activities that take place on a Sunday, especially retail activity.

bounce
to write a check when you do not have enough money in your account to cover it.

brand name
brand-name products are made by famous national manufacturers and are familiar to most people through advertising. ⇨ **store brand.**

buck
an informal word for a dollar. It can also be used in the plural: "It cost ten/twenty-five/seven hundred bucks."

bulk
things sold "in bulk" are sold in large sizes or in multiple packs, rather than as individual items.

cash register
a machine that adds up purchases and holds money; *till*.

catalog
a magazine that contains a selection of products that can be ordered by phone or mail and delivered to the buyer by mail or other delivery service.

checking account
a bank account that allows clients to withdraw money, either by the use of checks or through ATMs; *current account.*

checkout
in stores, the place where shoppers pay for their purchases.

convenience store
a small store that sells a limited range of goods and some ready-to-eat foods, such as 7-Eleven; *corner shop.*

department store
a large store that sells a wide variety of merchandise organized into separate departments.

deposit
to put money into a bank account; *pay in.*

dime
a small, thin, silver-colored U.S. coin worth ten cents.

discount retailer
a large store that sells all kinds of products at low prices.

drugstore
a store that fills prescriptions and sells other medications but also stocks a variety of other goods, such as health and beauty products, stationery, small electrical appliances, and candy. Some drugstores also carry a selection of basic food items.

dry goods
merchandise such as clothing, fabrics, and related goods.

e-auction
an electronic auction carried out over the Internet.

express mail
a category of mail for letters that need to arrive overnight.

food court
an area in a shopping mall that has a number of different fast-food counters with a common seating area in the middle.

grocery (store)
a supermarket.

half-dollar
a silver-colored U.S. coin worth fifty cents.

hardware store
a store that sells tools and other objects that might be necessary around the house; *ironmonger*.

home improvement
the American term for *DIY*.

infomercial
a TV show that is not aired regularly, the object of which is to sell a product. They feature repeated demonstrations of all the amazing things that the product can do as well as long speeches from satisfied customers. Minor celebrities are sometimes used to help sell a product.

Laundromat
a place with coin-operated washing machines and dryers that the public can use; *launderette*.

liquor store
a store that sells alcoholic beverages; *off-licence*.

mail
items such as letters and packages that are sent through the postal service; *post*.

mailbox
a container placed in a public area in which people can deposit mail to be sent; *postbox*. It's also a private container in which people can receive mail; *letterbox*.

mail carrier
a person who delivers mail; *postman*.

mailman
a **mail carrier.**

mail order
a way of shopping by ordering things either from a catalog or from TV.

mass merchandiser
another term for a **discount retailer.**

mini-mart
another word for a **convenience store.**

money order
a document like a check that you can buy from a post office and use instead of a check. If you are sending a payment through the mail, you must use a money order or a check, not cash.

newsstand
a kiosk from which newspapers and magazines are sold.

nickel
a U.S. coin worth five cents. It is made of a nickel and copper alloy and is quite thick.

no-frills
used to describe a store that has little or no decorations, has no special customer services such as home deliveries and fitting rooms, and which charges very low prices.

outlet (store)
a store that sells merchandise at a reduced price. Outlets are often found grouped together in outlet malls outside of cities.

overhead
the costs to a store for renting or owning a building, including heat, lighting, and property taxes.

package store
a store that sells sealed alcoholic beverages that are to be drunk elsewhere.

penny
a small copper U.S. coin worth one cent. It is the only copper coin used in the United States.

plus size
a nice way to say "large clothing for overweight people."

post office
the place where people go to buy stamps and send letters and packages; post offices also have post office boxes available for people to rent.

produce
fresh fruit and vegetables. A *greengrocer's* is a **produce stand.**

quarter
a thin, silver-colored U.S. coin worth twenty-five cents. It is used in most vending machines and coin-operated machines.

ring up
to use a cash register to add up the cost of the goods that someone is buying, and take the customer's payment. The term comes from the noise made by early cash registers.

salesperson/sales assistant
someone who sells merchandise in a store; *shop assistant*.

SASE
self-addressed stamped envelope; an envelope with your address and a stamp on it that you send to a company so that they can send information back to you; *SAE*.

savings account
a bank account that pays interest on money you have saved. Access to the money in savings accounts may be subject to restrictions.

shipping and handling (S&H)
an amount of money that is paid to cover the delivery of merchandise ordered by mail or over the phone or Internet; *postage and packing*.

shopping cart
a metal cart with a large basket for putting purchases in while doing shopping; *shopping trolley*.

special delivery
a method of sending mail more quickly and safely by special messenger that costs a little extra; *recorded delivery*.

store brand
a product that is made for a particular store. These products are usually very similar to **brand name** products but cost less.

strip mall
a shopping area that consists of a single row of stores with a parking lot in front.

superstore

originally, a very large supermarket that sells food and other groceries and also stocks a wide variety of nonfood products, such as electronic equipment, clothes, sporting goods, and hardware items. The word is now applied to any very large store of any kind, especially one that stocks more than one specific type of item.

thrift store

a store that sells secondhand clothes and furniture. Thrift stores are sometimes, but not always, run by charities.

warehouse club

very large stores, usually located in warehouses, that charge an annual membership fee but allow members to save much more than their fee because of the large discounts they offer.

ZIP code

a five-digit code placed at the end of an address (after the state name) that helps the Postal Service sort and deliver mail; *postcode.*

👉 Key Confusables and Americanisms:

This whole chapter is about confusable American things, so we'll skip this bit.

👉 Key Grammar:

Not much here. But Americans usually say, "What size shoe do you wear?" rather than "What size shoe do you take?"

👉 Key Cultural Points:

The average American lives in blissful ignorance of the metric system, even though metric equivalents have commonly been printed on most products for several years now. It is, however, used in the scientific, construction, and engineering industries.

While units in the U.S. Customary System may have the same names as those in the British Imperial System, the measures are not always the same! So, for example, an American pint is four ounces less than a British one.

· ·

Weights and Measures

American weight measurements are based on **avoirdupois weight**—a system of measurement based on a pound being equal to sixteen ounces. The "stone" is not used at all in the United States. The average American would be more likely to know his or her weight in kilos than to have any idea of what a stone is, and Americans don't know kilos.

The abbreviation for "pound" is **lb.**, from the Latin word *libra*, which is also where the British get the L with a cross through it that is the symbol for their money—pounds. The abbreviation for "ounce" is **oz.**

The following table shows how to convert metric amounts into U.S. equivalents:

Metric units	multiply by	to obtain
grams	0.035	ounces
kilograms	2.2	pounds
metric tons (1,000 kg)	1.1	short tons (2,000 lbs.)
millimeters	0.04	inches
centimeters	0.39	inches
meters	3.28	feet
	1.09	yards
kilometers	0.62	miles
milliliters	0.2	teaspoons
	0.06	tablespoons
	0.03	fluid ounces
liters	1.06	quarts
	0.26	gallons
	4.23	cups
	2.12	pints
cubic meters	35.32	cubic feet
square centimeters	0.16	square inches
square meters	1.2	square yards
square kilometers	0.39	square miles

To convert U.S. measures to metric:

U.S. measures	multiply by	to obtain
ounces	28.35	grams
pounds	0.45	kilograms
short tons (2,000 lbs.)	0.91	metric tons
inches	25.4	millimeters
	2.54	centimeters
feet	30.48	centimeters
yards	0.91	meters
miles	1.61	kilometers
teaspoons	4.93	milliliters
tablespoons	14.79	milliliters
fluid ounces	29.57	milliliters
cups	0.24	liters

(continued)

U.S. measures	multiply by	to obtain
pints	0.47	liters
quarts	0.95	liters
gallons	3.79	liters
cubic feet	0.028	cubic meters
cubic yards	0.76	cubic meters
square inches	6.45	square centimeters
square feet	0.09	square meters
square yards	0.84	square meters
square miles	2.6	square kilometers

As we said, certain American measures of capacity do not correspond to Imperial measures with the same names:

U.S.	Imperial
1 pint (16 oz.)	0.83 pints
1 quart (32 oz.)	1.66 pints
1 gallon (64 oz.)	0.83 gallons

In addition, the American tablespoon is slightly smaller than the Imperial one. The dessertspoon is not used as a measurement in the United States. The closest thing to it is a **teaspoon.**

Temperatures

Americans use the Fahrenheit scale to measure temperature. To convert a temperature in Celsius to Fahrenheit:

multiply by 1.8, then add 32

To convert a temperature in Fahrenheit to Celsius:

subtract 32, then divide by 1.8

An easy way to at least have some idea of the temperature is to remember that 28 degrees Celsius is 82 Fahrenheit, and 16 Celsius is 61 Fahrenheit. The others to remember are 32 degrees (freezing) and 212 degrees (boiling).

WEIGHTS & MEASURES

Paper Sizes

If you say "A4," Americans will give you a funny look. Paper sizes do not have names, they have numbers, and the numbers are not metric. The standard paper size is called **letter size** and is $8\frac{1}{2} \times 11$ inches, which is a little shorter and fatter than A4. **Legal size** is $8\frac{1}{4} \times 14$, and a large sheet is usually 11×17. Anyone who has been e-mailed a document from America and tried to print it will already be familiar with the paper size problem.

Clothing Sizes

American clothing manufacturers use either numbers or the terms **small, medium, large,** and **extra large** in their sizes. These are different from those used in Britain and Europe. In general, American clothes are cut somewhat larger than in other countries, so it is best to try clothes on rather than just go by conversion tables.

Women's Sizes

U.S.	4	6	8	10	12	14	16	18	20	22
U.K.		8	10	12	14	16	18	20	22	24
Europe		34	36	38	40	42	44	46	48	50
	small (S)		medium (M)			large (L)		extra large (XL)		extra extra large (XXL)

Women's Shoes

U.S.	4	5	6	7	8	9	10	11
U.K.	2	3	4	5	6	7	8	9
Europe	35	36	37	38	39	40	41	42

WEIGHTS & MEASURES

Men's Sizes

	S		M		L	XL	XXL
U.S.							
U.K.	34	36	38	40	42	44	46
Europe	44	46	48	50	52	54	56

The above measurements correspond to casual and sportswear. Men's suits are sized by chest measurement, and shirt sizes correspond to neck size and arm length, so it is best to be measured by the sales assistant in the store. Most stores offer this service. Pants are sized according to waist size and inseam length.

Men's Shoes

U.S.	4	5	6	7	8	9	10	11	12
U.K.	3	4	5	6	7	8	9	10	11
Europe	35	36	37	39	40	41	42	44	46

Children's Sizes

U.S.	2	4	6	8	10	12
U.K.	16/18	20/22	24/26	28/30	32/34	36/38
Europe	92	104	116	128	140	152

S, M, L, and XL sizes are also used for children's clothes.

Pronunciation Symbols for the Sounds of American English

Stress

/ˈ/	/ˈpɝsən/	**PER**son	Primary stress—goes
	/pɚˈsɛnt/	per**CENT**	above the line before the strongest syllable in a word
/ˌ/	/ˈnuzˌpeɪpɚ/	NEWS**pa**per	Secondary stress—goes
	/ˌɪnfɚˈmeɪʃən/	**in**for**MA**tion	below the line before the second strongest syllable in a word

Vowels (arranged phonetically)

/i/	**ea**t, s**ee**, n**ee**d
/ɪ/	**i**t, b**i**g, f**i**nishes
/eɪ/	**ai**d, d**ay**, h**a**te
/ɛ/	**e**ver, h**ea**d, g**e**t
/æ/	**a**pple, b**a**d, h**a**t
/ɑ/	**o**dd, f**a**ther, h**o**t
/ʌ/	**u**p, m**o**ther, m**u**d *(in stressed syllables)*
/ə/	**a**bout, anim**a**l, probl**e**m, pol**i**te, s**u**ggest, ser**iou**s *(in unstressed syllables)*
/ɔ/	**a**ll, s**aw**, t**a**lk, c**au**ght
/oʊ/	**ow**e, r**oa**d, h**o**pe
/ʊ/	g**oo**d, b**oo**k, p**u**t
/u/	t**oo**, f**oo**d, s**ou**p
/aɪ/	**I**, h**i**de, r**igh**t
/aʊ/	**ou**t, h**ow**, l**ou**d
/ɔɪ/	**oi**l, t**oy**, ch**oi**ce
/ɝ/	**ear**ly, h**er**, b**ir**d, h**ur**t *(in stressed syllables)*
/ɝ/	c**ur**ry, st**irr**ing *(in stressed syllables, where /r/ is followed by a vowel)*
/ɚ/	teach**er**, doct**or**, pict**ure**, aft**erward** *(in unstressed syllables)*

/ər/	liter**a**l, summ**a**rize *(in unstressed syllables, where /**r**/ is followed by a vowel)*
/ɪr/	**ear**, b**eer**
/ɛr/	**air**, c**are**
/ar/	**ar**m, f**ar**
/ɔr/	**or**der, m**ore**
/ʊr/	p**ure**, t**our**
/aɪr/	f**ire**, t**ire**d
/aʊr/	h**our**
/əl/	bott**le**, met**al**, chann**el**
/ən/	butt**on**, sudd**en**, mount**ain**

Consonants (arranged alphabetically, with special symbols last)

/b/	**b**oy, **b**a**b**y, ro**b**
/d/	**d**o, la**dd**er, be**d**
/f/	**f**ood, o**ff**er, sa**fe**
/g/	**g**et, bi**gg**er, do**g**
/h/	**h**appy, a**h**ead
/k/	**c**an, spea**k**er, sti**ck**
/l/	**l**et, fo**ll**ow, sti**ll**
/m/	**m**ake, su**mm**er, ti**m**e
/n/	**n**o, di**nn**er, thi**n**
/ŋ/	si**ng**er, thi**n**k, lo**ng**
/p/	**p**ut, a**pp**le, cu**p**
/r/	**r**un, ma**rr**y, fa**r**, sto**r**e
/s/	**s**it, pa**ss**ing, **c**ity, fa**ce**
/t/	**t**op, be**tt**er, ca**t**
/v/	**v**ery, se**v**en, lo**v**e
/w/	**w**ear, **wh**ere, a**w**ay
/hw/	**wh**ere, some**wh**at
/x/	**Ch**anukah, lo**ch**
/y/	**y**es, **u**se, be**y**ond
/z/	**z**oo, bu**zz**, ea**s**y, plea**s**e
/θ/	**th**irsty, no**th**ing, ma**th**
/ð/	**th**is, mo**th**er, brea**the**
/ʃ/	**sh**e, sta**ti**on, pu**sh**
/tʃ/	**ch**urch, wat**ch**ing, na**t**ure
/ʒ/	mea**s**ure, televi**s**ion, bei**ge**
/dʒ/	**j**ump, bu**dg**et, a**ge**

Word Converter

U.S. Term	Pronunciation	British Equivalent
about (=approximately)	/əˈbaʊt/	round about
absorb	/əbˈsɔrb/	take up
accordion	/əˈkɔrdiən/	concertina
acetominophen	/əˌsitəˈmɪnəfən/	paracetamol
achy	/ˈeɪki/	achey
acidic	/əˈsɪdɪk/	acid (adj.)
acknowledgment	/əkˈnɑlɪdʒmənt/	acknowledgement
addition sign	/əˈdɪʃən ˌsaɪn/	add sign
adds	/ædz/	adds up
advertisements, ads (on TV)	/ˌædvərˈtaɪzmənts/ /ædz/	adverts
aerie	/ˈɛri/	eyrie
after (the hour, as in "It's five after eight.")	/ˈæftɚ/	past ("It's five past eight.")
afterward	/ˈæftɚwɚd/	afterwards
aging	/ˈeɪdʒɪŋ/	ageing
ahead	/əˈhɛd/	in front
air bag	/ˈɛr ˌbæg/	airbag
aircraft	/ˈɛrˌkræft/	aeroplane
airfoil	/ˈɛrˌfɔɪl/	aerofoil
airplane	/ˈɛrˌpleɪn/	aeroplane
aisle	/aɪl/	gangway
alfalfa sprouts	/ælˈfælfə ˌspraʊts/	cress (the tiny plants that are not hot)
all-around (adj.)	/ˈɔl əˈraʊnd/	all-round
all right	/ˌɔl ˈraɪt/	alright

193

U.S. Term	Pronunciation	British Equivalent
all year/day/week long		all year/day/week round
alligator clip	/ˈælɪˌɡeɪtɚ ˈklɪp/	crocodile clip
all-purpose flour	/ˈɔl ˌpɚpəs ˈflaʊr/	plain flour
alto recorder	/ˈæltoʊ rɪˈkɔrdɚ/	treble recorder
aluminum	/əˈlumənəm/	aluminium
among		amongst
amusement park	/əˈmyuzmənt ˌpɑrk/	leisure park
analyze	/ˈænəˌlaɪz/	analyse
anchor,	/ˈæŋkɚ/	newsreader
anchorman,	/ˈæŋkɚˌmən/	
anchorwoman	/ˈæŋkɚˌwʊmən/	
anesthetic	/ˌænəsˈθetɪk/	anaesthetic
angry	/ˈæŋgri/	cross (adj.)
ankle bracelet	/ˈæŋkəl ˌbreɪslɪt/	anklet
anklets (= short socks)	/ˈæŋklɪts/	ankle socks
Antarctic Ocean	/ænˈtɑrktɪk ˈoʊʃən/	Southern Ocean
antenna (on a television)	/ænˈtenə/	aerial
anymore	/ˌeniˈmɔr/	any more
apartment	/əˈpɑrtmənt/	flat
apartment building	/əˈpɑrtmənt ˌbɪldɪŋ/	block of flats
appetizer	/ˈæpɪˌtaɪzɚ/	starter
archeology,	/ˌɑrkiˈɑlədʒi/	archaeology
archaeology	/ˌɑrkiˈɑlədʒi/	
area code (telephone)	/ˈɛriə ˌkoʊd/	code number
armoire	/ɑrmˈwɑr/	wardrobe
armor	/ˈɑrmɚ/	armour
around (e.g., wander around)	/əˈraʊnd/	about (e.g., wander about)
around (e.g., Do you live around here?; around 10%)		round, round about (e.g., Do you live round here?; round about 10%)
artifact	/ˈɑrtəˌfækt/	artefact
arts & crafts store	/ˈɑrts ən ˈkræfts ˌstɔr/	art supply shop
athletic	/æθˈletɪk/	sporty
ATM, automated teller machine	/ˈoʊtəmeɪtɪd ˈtelɚ məˌʃin/	cash dispenser, cashpoint

U.S. Term	Pronunciation	British Equivalent
attic	/ˈætɪk/	loft
attorney (*in a court*)	/əˈtɜrni/	barrister
attorney (*outside a court*)		solicitor
automobile	/ɔtəməˈbil/	motor car
avid	/ˈævɪd/	keen
awkward	/ˈɔkwəd/	fiddly
ax	/æks/	axe
baby basket/carrier	/ˈbeibi ˌbæskɪt/	carry-cot
baby buggy/carriage	/ˈbeibi ˌkæriə/	pram
	/ˈbeibi ˌbʌgi/	
	/ˈbeibi ˌkærɪdʒ/	
back and forth	/ˈbæk ən ˈfɔrθ/	backwards and forwards
backpack	/ˈbækˌpæk/	rucksack
back road	/ˈbæk ˌroud/	byway
back-up lights	/ˈbæk ʌp ˌlaɪts/	reversing lights
backward (*adv.*)	/ˈbækwəd/	backwards
backyard	/ˈbækˈyard/	garden
baggage	/ˈbægɪdʒ/	luggage
baggage car (*on a train*)	/ˈbægɪdʒ ˌkar/	luggage van
baked potato	/ˈbeikt pəˌteitou/	jacket potato
baking soda	/ˈbeikɪŋ ˌsoudə/	bicarbonate of soda
balcony (*in a theater*)	/ˈbælkəni/	gallery
ball cock	/ˈbɔl ˈkɔk/	float valve
ballot paper	/ˈbælət ˌpeipə/	voting paper
ballpoint (*pen*)	/ˈbɔlˌpɔint ˈpen/	ball point pen, biro
band (*circular*)	/bænd/	ring
Band-Aid™	/ˈbænd ˌeid/	Elastoplast™, (sticking) plaster
bangs (*hair*)	/bæŋz/	fringe
banquet hall	/ˈbæŋkwɪt ˌhɔl/	banqueting hall
bark (*boat*)	/bark/	barque
bar owner	/ˈbar ˌounə/	landlord (*of a pub*)
barrette	/bəˈret/	hair slide
bartender	/ˈbarˌtendə/	barman
baseboard	/ˈbeisˌbɔrd/	skirting board

U.S. Term	Pronunciation	British Equivalent
basement apartment	/'beɪsmənt ə'pɑrtmənt/	garden flat
bathe	/beɪð/	bath (*verb*)
bathing; taking a bath	/'beɪðɪŋ/	having a bath
bathroom; *also half bathroom, guest bathroom, hall bathroom*	/'hæf 'bæθˌrum/, /'gest 'bæθˌrum/, /'hɔl 'bæθˌrum/	loo, WC, toilet, lavatory, cloakroom
bathtub	/'bæθˌtʌb/	bath (*noun*)
batting	/'bætɪŋ/	wadding
beet	/bit/	beetroot
behavior	/bɪ'heɪvyɚ/	behaviour
bellhop, bellboy	/'belˌhɑp/, /'belˌbɔɪ/	hotel porter
bell captain	/'bel ˌkæptən/	head porter (*in a hotel*)
bell station	/'bel ˌsteɪʃən/	(=*a place in a hotel where you can get help with your luggage and taxis*)
not belong		be the odd one out
besides	/bɪ'saɪdz/	apart from
bicycle riding, bike rider	/'baɪsɪkəl ˌraɪdɪŋ/, /'baɪk ˌraɪdɚ/	cycling, cyclist
Big Dipper	/'bɪg 'dɪpɚ/	Plough (*constellation*)
bill (*money*)	/bɪl/	bank note
billboard	/'bɪlˌbɔrd/	a hoarding
billfold	/'bɪlˌfoʊld/	purse, wallet
biplane	/'baɪˌpleɪn/	bi-plane
blanks (*fill in the...*)	/blæŋks/	gaps
blind (*for bird watchers*)	/blaɪnd/	hide
(Venetian) blinds (=*slatted ones for windows*)	/və'niʃən 'blaɪndz/	blind
blob	/blɑb/	splodge
blocks (*children's*)	/blɑks/	bricks
bobby pin	/'bɑbi ˌpɪn/	hair grip, kirby grip
bobsled	/'bɑbˌslɛd/	bobsleigh
to a boil, to boiling point		to the boil
! bomb (=*failure*)	/bɑm/	bomb (=*success*)
border	/'bɔrdɚ/	frontier

U.S. Term	Pronunciation	British Equivalent
bottle return	/ˈbɑtəl rɪˌtɜ˞n/	bottle bank
bouillon cube	/ˈbʊlyən ˌkyub/	stock cube
boutonniere	/ˌbutɪˈnir/	buttonhole
braid	/breɪd/	plait
break (=short vacation)	/breɪk/	holiday, half-term
briefs	/brifs/	Y-fronts
bring ("fetch" is for dogs only)	/brɪŋ/	fetch
broad jump	/ˈbrɔd ˌdʒʌmp/	long jump
broil	/brɔɪl/	grill (verb)
broiler	/ˈbrɔɪlə˞/	grill (noun)
broth	/brɔθ/	stock
brush your teeth		clean your teeth
! bugger (=a young boy, as in "a cute little bugger")	/ˈbʌgə˞/	(This does not mean sodomy in the U.S.)
built-in cupboards	/ˈbɪlt ɪn ˈkʌbə˞dz/	fitted cupboards
bulletin board	/ˈbʊlɪtən ˌbɔrd/	noticeboard
bump (noun)	/bʌmp/	knock
bumper car	/ˈbʌmpə˞ ˌkɑr/	dodgem car
bumpers (railroad)	/ˈbʌmpə˞z/	buffers
bun (for hamburgers)	/bʌn/	bap (British "bun"=U.S. "sweet roll")
bureau (furniture)	/ˈbyʊrou/	chest of drawers
burglarized	/ˈbɜ˞gləˌraɪzd/	burgled
burlap	/ˈbɜ˞læp/	hessian
burned (adj., past tense)	/bɜ˞nd/	burnt
burners (on a stove)	/ˈbɜ˞nə˞z/	rings
bus	/bʌs/	coach
busboy, busser	/ˈbʌsˌbɔɪ/, /ˈbʌsə˞/	kitchen porter
business suit	/ˈbɪznɪs ˌsut/	lounge suit
busy (phone)	/ˈbɪzi/	engaged
buzzard	/ˈbʌzə˞d/	vulture
buzz saw	/ˈbʌz ˌsɔ/	circular saw
cabinet (in kitchen; "cupboard" is also used)	/ˈkæbənɪt/ /ˈkʌbə˞d/	cupboard

U.S. Term	Pronunciation	British Equivalent
caboose (on a train)	/kəˈbus/	guard's van
cake (not little cakes)	/keɪk/	sponge, gâteau
cupcakes	/ˈkʌpˌkeɪks/	cakes
caldron	/ˈkɔldrən/	cauldron
(personal) calendar	/ˈpɜːsənəl ˌkæləndɚ/	diary
(wall) calendar	/ˈwɔl ˌkæləndɚ/	wall planner
call (phone)	/kɔl/	ring
call collect	/ˈkɔl kəˈlɛkt/	reverse the charges
camper (vehicle)	/ˈkæmpɚ/	caravan
campfire	/ˈkæmpˌfaɪr/	camp fire
can	/kæn/	tin
canceled, canceling	/ˈkænsəld/, /ˈkænsəlɪŋ/	cancelled, cancelling
candy cane	/ˈkændi ˌkeɪn/	candy stick
candy store	/ˈkændi ˌstɔr/	sweetshop, confectioner
candy, a piece of candy	/ˈkændi/	sweets, a sweet
canola oil	/kəˈnoʊlə ˌɔɪl/	rapeseed oil
capital letters	/ˈkæpɪtəl ˌlɛtɚz/	capitals
car	/kar/	motor car
car (on a train)		carriage
car racing	/ˈkar ˌreɪsɪŋ/	motor racing
(a) caramel	/ˈkærəməl/, /ˈkarˌməl/	(a) toffee
carburetor	/ˈkarbəˌreɪtɚ/	carburettor
carcass	/ˈkarkəs/	carcasse
cardboard	/ˈkardˌbɔrd/	card
cargo ship	/ˈkargoʊ ˌʃɪp/	transportation ship
carnival	/ˈkarnəvəl/	fair
carpenter	/ˈkarpəntɚ/	joiner
carpentry	/ˈkarpəntri/	joinery
carry (in a store)	/ˈkæri/, /ˈkeri/	stock
cash register	/ˈkæʃ ˌrɛdʒəstɚ/	till
casket (if elaborate)	/ˈkæskɪt/	coffin
catalog (noun, verb)	/ˈkætəˌlɔg/	catalogue
centennial	/sɛnˈtɛniəl/	centenary
center	/ˈsɛntɚ/	centre
cesspool	/ˈsɛsˌpul/	cesspit

U.S. Term	Pronunciation	British Equivalent
chase off	/ˌtʃeɪs 'ɔf/	see off
! cheap (=*"of low quality"* as well as *"inexpensive"*)	/tʃip/	cheap (=*inexpensive*)
check (*in a restaurant*)	/tʃɛk/	bill
check (*from a bank account*)	/tʃɛk/	cheque
check mark	/'tʃɛk ˌmɑrk/	tick
check off, check something off	/ˌtʃɛk 'ɔf/	tick off, make a tick
checked (=*regular pattern only*)	/tʃɛkt/	checked (=*regular pattern or tartan*)
checkered	/'tʃɛkə-d/	chequered
checkers	/'tʃɛkə-z/	draughts
checking account	/'tʃɛkɪŋ əˌkaʊnt/	current account
cheekbone	/'tʃik,boʊn/	cheek-bone
cheesecloth	/'tʃiz,klɔθ/	muslin
chew out	/ˌtʃu 'aʊt/	tell off
chief counsel (*in court*)	/'tʃif 'kaʊnsəl/	leader
chilies/chili	/'tʃɪliz/, /'tʃɪli/	chillies/chilli
chilly	/'tʃɪli/	chill (*adj.*)
china cabinet	/'tʃaɪnə ˌkæbənɪt/	dresser
chips	/tʃɪps/	crisps
cigarette	/ˌsɪgə'rɛt/	fag, ciggy
cinnamon roll	/'sɪnəmən ˌroʊl/	Chelsea bun
circle (*noun, verb*)	/'sɜ-kəl/	ring (*noun*) circle (*verb*)
cleats (*soccer*)	/klits/	studs (*football*)
clergyman	/'klɜ-dʒimən/	vicar
! clever	/'klɛvə-/	too clever; slightly suspicious; crafty
clipped	/klɪpt/	snipped
closet (*if built-in*)	/'klazɪt/	cupboard
clothes basket	/'kloʊz ˌbæskɪt/	linen basket, washing basket
clothesline	/'kloʊz,laɪn/	washing line
clothespin	/'kloʊz,pɪn/	clothes-peg
! cock	/kak/	slang for a penis (Americans do not say "willy.")

U.S. Term	Pronunciation	British Equivalent
coffee with cream/milk	/'kafi/	white coffee
collarbone	/'kalə‚boʊn/	collar-bone
colleagues	/'kaligz/	work mates
in college/school	/'kalıdʒ/, /‚skul/	at university
color	/'kʌlə/	colour
colorblind	/'kʌlə‚blaınd/	colour blind
colored	/'kʌləd/	coloured
comforter	/'kʌmfətə/	duvet
commercial (*on TV*)	/kə'mɚʃəl/	advert
complain	/kəm'pleın/	grizzle, whinge
complete (*sentence*)	/kəm'plit/	whole (*sentence*)
complete (*for emphasis, as in "a complete idiot"*)		right ("*a right idiot*")
completely (*e.g., completely finished*)	/kəm'plitli/	quite (*quite finished*)
concert master (*1ˢᵗ violin*)	/'kansət ‚mæstə/	leader
conclusive	/kən'klusıv/	damning
conductor (*railroad*)	/kən'dʌktə/	guard
cone (*for ice cream*)	/koʊn/	cornet
confectioners' sugar	/kən'fekʃənəz 'ʃʊgə/	icing sugar
connect (*phone*)	/kə'nekt/	put through
construction paper (*for art projects*)	/kən'strʌkʃən ‚peıpə/	card
continue (*doing something*)	/kən'tınyu/	carry on
cookbook	/'kʊk‚bʊk/	cookery book
cookie	/'kʊki/	biscuit (*sweet*)
cookie sheet	/'kʊki ʃit /	baking tray
cooler	/'kulə/	cool box
cooperate	/koʊ'apə‚reıt/	co-operate
coordinate (*verb*)	/koʊ'ɔrdə‚neıt/	co-ordinate
cop (*police*)	/kap/	copper, Bobby (*in London*)
copy editor	/'kapi ‚edıtə/	subeditor
cord elastic	/'kɔrd ı‚læstık/	hat elastic
corn	/kɔrn/	maize
corn		sweetcorn

U.S. Term	Pronunciation	British Equivalent
corned beef (=beef that has been preserved in brine and slowly cooked)	/'kɔrnd 'bif/	corned beef (=processed meat)
cornstarch	/'kɔrn,startʃ/	cornflour
corn syrup	/'kɔrn ,sɪrəp/	(No real equivalent; a bit like golden syrup, only lighter.)
correspondence course	/,kɔrə'spandəns ,kɔrs/	distance learning course
costume (party)	/'kastum/	fancy dress (party)
cot	/kat/	camp bed
cotton candy	/'katən 'kændi/	candy floss
cotton; cotton balls	/'katən/, /'katən ,bɔlz/	cotton wool
couldn't have known		wasn't to know
counselor	/'kaʊnsələ/	counsellor
counterclockwise	/,kaʊntə'klak,waɪz/	anti-clockwise
counting	/'kaʊntɪŋ/	counting up
country club	/'kʌntri ,klʌb/	golf club
cracker	/'krækə/	biscuit (savory)
get a cramp (in your leg, etc.) get/have cramps (menstrual)	/kræmp/	get cramp
crawfish, crayfish	/'krɔ,fɪʃ/, /'kreɪ,fɪʃ/	crayfish
crazy	/'kreɪzi/	mad
cream of wheat	/'krim əv 'wit/	semolina
crib	/krɪb/	cot
crisscrossed	/'krɪs,krɔst/	criss-crossed
crossbred	/'krɔs,brɛd/	cross-bred
crossing guard	/'krɔsɪŋ ,gard/	lollipop lady
crosswalk	/'krɔs,wɔk/	zebra crossing
crumpled up (paper)	/'krʌmpəld 'ʌp/	screwed up
cuffs (trousers)	/kʌfs/	turn-ups
curb (edge of sidewalk)	/kɝb/	kerb
cursive	/'kɝsɪv/	joined-up writing
custom-made	/'kʌstəm 'meɪd/	made-to-measure; bespoke
cut in line		jump the queue

WORD CONVERTER

U.S. Term	Pronunciation	British Equivalent
dashboard, dash (*on a car*)	/ˈdæʃˌbɔrd/, /dæʃ/	fascia panel
dead battery	/ˈdɛd ˈbætəri/	flat battery
dear (*=beloved*)	/dɪr/	dear (*=expensive*)
deck (*of cards*)	/dɛk/	pack
decorating tip	/ˈdɛkəˌreɪtɪŋ ˌtɪp/	icing nozzle
deep bowl		pudding basin
defense	/dɪˈfɛns/ (*in sports*) /ˈdiˌfɛns/	defence
delivery truck	/dɪˈlɪvəri ˌtrʌk/	van
denatured alcohol	/diˈneɪtʃəd ˈælkəˌhɔl/	methylated spirits
derby	/ˈdɜbi/	bowler
desk clerk ("*receptionist*" is also used)	/ˈdɛsk ˌklɜk/	receptionist
dessert	/dɪˈzɜt/	pudding, afters, sweet
detour	/ˈditʊr/	diversion
dialing	/ˈdaɪəlɪŋ/	dialling
diaper	/ˈdaɪpə/	nappy
diarrhea	/ˌdaɪəˈriə/	diarrhoea
diary (*=journal*)	/ˈdaɪəri/	diary (*=personal calendar*)
! dick (*DO NOT use this word. There is no such thing as "spotted dick" in the U.S.*)		penis; wanker
a die ("*dice*" is plural)	/daɪ/, /daɪs/	a dice
dike	/daɪk/	dyke
dimmed (*lights*)	/dɪmd/	dipped (*lights*)
dinner	/ˈdɪnə/	tea (*meal*)
dinner roll	/ˈdɪnə ˌroʊl/	bread roll
dinner table	/ˈdɪnə ˌteɪbəl/	meal table
directory assistance	/dɪˈrɛktəri əˌsɪstəns/	directory inquiries
dirigible	/ˈdɪrɪdʒəbəl/	airship
dirt	/dɜt/	earth
discoveries	/dɪˈskʌvəriz/	findings
dishes	/ˈdɪʃɪz/	crockery
the dishes, do the dishes		the washing up, do the washing up

U.S. Term	Pronunciation	British Equivalent
disgrace	/dɪsˈgreɪs/	dishonour
dishonor	/dɪsˈɑnɚ/	dishonour
be dismissed	/dɪsˈmɪst/	get the sack
dishwasher	/ˈdɪʃˌwɑʃɚ/	washer-upper
dishwashing detergent	/ˈdɪʃˌwɑʃɪŋ dɪˈtɚdʒənt/	washing-up liquid
disk	/dɪsk/	disc (*not computer*)
dispatch	*verb* /dɪˈspætʃ; *noun also* /ˈdɪspætʃ/	despatch
dishwashing detergent bottle		squeezy bottle
distribute	/dɪˈstrɪbyut/	share out
divided highway	/dɪˈvaɪdɪd ˈhaɪˌweɪ/	dual carriageway
dock	/dɑk/	quay
doghouse	/ˈdɔgˌhaʊs/	kennel
dollhouse	/ˈdɑlˌhaʊs/	doll's house
dorm, dormitory	/dɔrm/, /ˈdɔrmɪˌtɔri/	hall of residence
dotted, polka-dotted	/ˈdɑtɪd/, /ˈpoʊkə ˌdɑtɪd/	spotted
double whole note	/ˈdʌbəl ˈhoʊl ˌnoʊt/	breve
dove	/dʌv/	dived
downspout	/ˈdaʊnˌspaʊt/	drainpipe
downtown	/ˈdaʊnˈtaʊn/	centre (*business/city*)
draft (*military*)	/dræft/	conscription
draft (*beer*)	/dræft/	draught
drain	/dreɪn/	drain off
drapes (*but "lace curtains"*)	/dreɪps/	curtains
dreamed	/drimd/	dreamt
dresser	/ˈdrɛsɚ/	chest of drawers
driving	/ˈdraɪvɪŋ/	motoring
drop by		look in on someone
drugstore	/ˈdrʌgˌstɔr/	chemist's
drunk	/drʌŋk/	pissed
dry goods store	/ˈdraɪ ˌgʊdz ˌstɔr/	draper
dump (*verb, noun*)	/dʌmp/	tip
dump truck	/ˈdʌmp ˌtrʌk/	dumper truck, (quarry) tipper

U.S. Term	Pronunciation	British Equivalent
Dumpster™	/ˈdʌmpstər/	skip
dungeon	/ˈdʌndʒən/	dungeons
duplex	/ˈduplɛks/	semi-detached house
dust ruffle (on bed)	/ˈdʌst ˌrʌfəl/	valance
eager	/ˈigər/	keen
earache	/ˈɪrˌeɪk/	ear ache
earthmover	/ˈɜrθˌmuvər/	digger
egg carton	/ˈɛg ˌkɑrtən/	egg box
egg white	/ˈɛg ˌwaɪt/	white of egg
eggplant	/ˈɛgˌplænt/	aubergine
eighth note	/ˈeɪθ ˌnoʊt/	quaver
elastic thread	/ɪˈlæstɪk ˈθrɛd/	shirring elastic
electric heater	/ɪˈlɛktrɪk ˈhitər/	electric fire
electrical wire/cord	/ɪˈlɛktrɪkəl ˈwaɪr/, /kɔrd/	lead, flex
elevator	/ˈɛləˌveɪtər/	lift
Elmer's™/school glue		PVA glue
end up		finish up
endive	/ˈɛndaɪv/	chicory
engineer (train)	/ˌɛndʒəˈnɪr/	driver
enhance	/ɛnˈhæns/	show up
enroll, enrollment	/ɛnˈroʊl/, /ɛnˈroʊlmənt/	enrol, enrolment
enthusiastic	/ɛnˌθuziˈæstɪk/	keen
entrance	/ˈɛntrəns/	way in
entrée (of a meal)	/ˈɑntreɪ/	main course
erase	/ɪˈreɪs/	rub out
eraser	/ɪˈreɪsər/	rubber
Erector set	/ɪˈrɛktər ˌsɛt/	Meccano set
esophagus	/ɪˈsɑfəgəs/	oesophagus
et cetera	/ɛt ˈsɛtərə/	and so on
exchange for	/ɪksˈtʃeɪndʒ ˌfɔr/	change into
exit	/ˈɛgzɪt/	way out
expensive	/ɪkˈspɛnsɪv/	dear
fabric store ("haberdashery" is old-fashioned, and means "men's clothing and accessories")	/ˈfæbrɪk ˌstɔr/	haberdashery

U.S. Term	Pronunciation	British Equivalent
faculty (*academic*)	/ˈfækəlti/	staff
! fag (*DO NOT use this word. It is never used as slang for a cigarette.*)		homosexual
fair	/fɛr/	fete
fairly	/ˈfɛrli/	quite, rather
fall	/fɔl/	autumn
fall down		fall over
fan (*shape*)	/fæn/	concertina
! fanny (*=a polite word for "bottom"*)	/ˈfæni/	fanny (*=a woman's genitals. Use "bottom" rather than "fanny," and not "backside" or "bum."*)
far lane	/ˈfɑr ˌleɪn/	offside lane
farsighted	/ˈfɑrˈsaɪtɪd/	long-sighted
farther (*for physical distance*)	/ˈfɑrðɚ/	further
faucet	/ˈfɔsɪt/	tap
fava bean	/ˈfɑvə bin/	broad bean
favor	/ˈfeɪvɚ/	favour
favorite	/ˈfeɪvərɪt/	favourite
feces	/ˈfisiz/	faeces
fender (*on a car*)	/ˈfɛndɚ/	wing
fertilizer	/ˈfɜrtəˌlaɪzɚ/	fertiliser
festival	/ˈfɛstəvəl/	fete
fetus	/ˈfitəs/	foetus
fiber	/ˈfaɪbɚ/	fibre
fiberglass	/ˈfaɪbɚˌglæs/	fibreglass, glass fibre
field	/fild/	pitch
fight (*noun, verb; used for both verbal arguments and physical fights*)	/faɪt/	quarrel
figure	/ˈfɪgyɚ/	reckon
figure eight	/ˈfɪgyɚ ˈeɪt/	figure-of-eight
figure something out		work out something
filet	/fɪˈleɪ/	fillet

U.S. Term	*Pronunciation*	*British Equivalent*
fill (*a bottle/glass*) halfway	/fɪl/	half-fill (*a bottle/glass*)
find (*something that is hard to see*)	/faɪnd/	spot
find out more about something		(*give something a*) look in
be fired	/faɪrd/	get the sack
fire department	/'faɪr dɪ,partmənt/	fire brigade
fire drill	/'faɪr ,drɪl/	fire practice
fire someone (*from a job*)	/'faɪr/	sack someone
firefighter	/'faɪr,faɪtɚ/	fire-fighter
fireworks (*party*)	/'faɪr,wɝks/	firework party
first (*adv.*)	/fɝst/	firstly
first balcony	/'fɝst 'bælkəni/	upper circle
first floor	/'fɝst 'flɔr/	ground floor
first name	/'fɝst 'neɪm/	Christian name
fish market	/'fɪʃ ,markət/	fishmonger
fish stick	/'fɪʃ ,stɪk/	fish finger
fix	/fɪks/	mend
fjord	/fyɔrd/	fiord
flashbulb (*photography*)	/'flæʃ,bʌlb/	flashlight
flashlight	/'flæʃ,laɪt/	torch
flatbed truck	/'flæt,bed 'trʌk/	low-loader
flavor	/'fleɪvɚ/	flavour
flexible	/'fleksəbəl/	bendy
flier (*for a concert, party, etc.*)	/'flaɪɚ/	flyer
floor lamp	/'flɔr ,læmp/	standard lamp
flutist	/'flutɪst/	flautist
fog light	/'fag ,laɪt/	fog lamp
foolish	/'fulɪʃ/	daft
football	/'fʊt,bɔl/	American football
forever	/fɔr'evɚ/	for ever
forklift	/'fɔrk,lɪft/	fork-lift
formula (*for babies*)	/'fɔrmyələ/	baby milk
formulas	/'fɔrmyələz/	formulae
forward	/'fɔrwɚd/	forwards

U.S. Term	*Pronunciation*	*British Equivalent*
freeway	/'fri,weɪ/	motorway
freighter	/'freɪtə-/	transportation ship
freight truck	/'freɪt ,trʌk/	goods truck
fries/French fries	/fraɪz/	chips
frighten	/'fraɪtən/	give someone a fright
frighten off		see off
front desk (*hotel, office*)	/'frʌnt 'dɛsk/	reception
frost (*verb*); frosting (*noun*)	/frɔst/, /'frɔstɪŋ/	ice; icing
fulfill	/fʊl'fɪl/	fulfil
full (*sentence*)	/fʊl/	whole (*sentence*)
in the future		in future
galoshes	/gə'lɑʃɪz/	boots, wellies
garbage	/'gɑrbɪdʒ/	rubbish
garbage dump		rubbish dump
garbage truck		dustcart
garbage bag		bin liner
garbage can		dustbin
garbage collector	/'gɑrbɪdʒ kə,lɛktə-/	dustman
garter belt	/'gɑrtə- ,bɛlt/	suspenders
gas station	/'gæs ,steɪʃən/	garage, petrol station
gas/gasoline	/gæs/, /,gæsə'lin/	petrol
gas/water/electricity lines		mains
gear shift	/'gɪr ʃɪft/	gear lever
generator	/'dʒɛnə,reɪtə-/	dynamo
German shepherd	/'dʒɜ-mən 'ʃɛpə-d/	Alsatian
get along with someone		get on with someone
get around/get out		get about
get going		move off
give away (*also* get rid of)		get rid of
give off (*e.g. fumes*)		give out
glove compartment	/'glʌv kəm,pɑrtmənt/	glove box
gnawing	/'nɔɪŋ/	niggling
go ahead, go on		off you go
goal (*of a plan, activity, etc.*)	/goʊl/	aim

U.S. Term	Pronunciation	British Equivalent
go bad (*rotten*)		go off
go by (*a store, mall, etc.*)		call in to
go for, go get		fetch
go on/keep on doing something (*continue*)		carry on
go to bed early		have an early night
golden raisin	/ˈgoʊldən ˈreɪzɪn/	sultana
Good job!	/ˈgʊd ˈdʒab/	Well done!
goose bumps	/ˈgus ˌbʌmps/	goose pimples
grab bag	/ˈgræb ˌbæg/	lucky dip
grade (*evaluation in school*)	/greɪd/	mark
grade (*year in school*)		class, form
grade crossing	/ˈgreɪd ˌkrɔsɪŋ/	level crossing
grain (*crops*)	/greɪn/	corn
gravel	/ˈgrævəl/	loose chippings
gray	/greɪ/	grey
green beans	/ˈgrin ˌbinz/	french beans
green onion	/ˈgrin ˈʌnyən/	spring onion
green thumb	/ˈgrin ˌθʌm/	green fingers
greeting card	/ˈgritɪŋ ˌkard/	greetings card
come to grips (*with something*)		get to grips (*with something*)
grocery store	/ˈgroʊsəri ˌstɔr/, /ˈgroʊʃri ˌstɔr/	grocer's
to ground (*a wire*)	/graʊnd/	to earth
ground beef	/ˌgraʊnd ˈbif/	mince, minced meat
grueling	/ˈgruəlɪŋ/	gruelling
grumpy	/ˈgrʌmpi/	bad-tempered
guard (*a player*)	/gard/	mark
guard (*in prison*)		warder
gummi bears	/ˈgʌmi ˌbɛrz/	jelly babies
gynecology	/ˌgaɪnɪˈkalədʒi/	gynaecology
ha, ha!		hah, hah!
had	/hæd/	had got

U.S. Term	Pronunciation	British Equivalent
hair stylist ("hairdresser" is old-fashioned in the U.S.)	/ˈhɛr ˌstaɪlɪst/	hairdresser
half note	/ˈhæf ˌnoʊt/	minim
halftime	/ˈhæfˌtaɪm/	half-time
halfway	/ˈhæfweɪ/	half-way
Halloween	/ˌhælə'win/	Hallowe'en
hamburger	/ˈhæmˌbɜ·gə·/	mince, minced meat
hang up	/hæŋ ʊp/	ring off
happy as a lark		happy as a sandboy
harbor	/ˈharbə·/	harbour
hardware seller	/ˈhard,wɛr ˌsɛlə·/	ironmonger
hardware store	/ˈhard,wɛr ˌstɔr/	ironmongers
harmonica	/harˈmanɪkə/	mouth organ
hatch	/hætʃ/	hatch out
have	/hæv/	have got
to have nothing to do with something		to be nothing to do with something
hawk	/hɔk/	buzzard
headband	/ˈhɛdˌbænd/	Alice band, hairband
headlights	/ˈhɛdˌlaɪts/	headlamps
in heat (ready to mate)	/hit/	on heat
heavy cream	/ˈhɛvi ˌkrim/	double cream
hello	/hɛˈloʊ/	hallo, hullo
hemo-		haemo-
highway	/ˈhaɪˌweɪ/	motorway
hit (success)	/hɪt/	bomb
hodgepodge	/ˈhadʒˌpadʒ/	hotchpotch
homegrown	/ˈhoʊm'groʊn/	home-grown
! homely (=plain or ugly)	/ˈhoʊmli/	Use "homey" for the British meaning of "homely."
homemade	/ˈhoʊm'meɪd/	home-made
honk (a horn)	/haŋk/	hoot
honor	/ˈanə·/	honour
honorable	/ˈanərəbəl/	honourable

U.S. Term	*Pronunciation*	*British Equivalent*
hood *(of a car)*	/hʊd/	bonnet
hope chest	/'hoʊp ˌtʃɛst/	bottom drawer
horned	/hɔrnd/	horny
❗horny	/'hɔrni/	randy (*"Randy" is a nickname in the U.S.; "horny" does not mean good-looking.*)
horse trailer	/'hɔrs ˌtreɪlɚ/	horsebox
horseback riding	/'hɔrsbæk ˌraɪdɪŋ/	horse riding
hose, garden hose	/hoʊz/	hosepipe
host	/hoʊst/	presenter
hourglass	/'aʊɚˌglæs/	sandglass
housing project *(if state-funded)*	/'haʊzɪŋ ˌpradʒɛkt/	housing estate
humongous	/hyu'mʌŋgəs/	ginormous
humor	/'hyumɚ/	humour
hungry *(slightly hungry)*	/'hʌŋgri/	peckish
hutch	/hʌtʃ/	dresser
hydroelectric	/ˌhaɪdroʊɪ'lɛktrɪk/	hydro-electric
ice water	/aɪs 'wɔtɚ/	iced water
ignite	/ɪg'naɪt/	set light to
inexpensive	/ˌɪnɪk'spɛnsɪv/	cheap
information *(telephone)*	/ˌɪnfɚ'meɪʃən/	directory enquiries
infrared	/ˌɪnfrə'rɛd/	infra-red
inquire *(to ask)*	/ɪn'kwaɪr/	enquire
inquiry	/ɪn'kwaɪri/	enquiry
insane	/ɪn'seɪn/	mad
inside lane	/'ɪnˌsaɪd 'leɪn/	nearside lane
installment	/ɪn'stɔlmənt/	instalment
installment plan		hire purchase
interested in	/'ɪntəˌrɛstɪd/	keen on
intermission	/ˌɪntɚ'mɪʃən/	interval
internist *(doctor)*	/'ɪntɚnɪst/	GP
intersection	/ˌɪntɚ'sɛkʃən/	junction
intestine	/ɪn'tɛstɪn/	gut
inward	/'ɪnwɚd/	inwards

U.S. Term	Pronunciation	British Equivalent
-ish, *as in* bluish, greenish		bluey, greeny, etc. (*Avoid the -ish suffix as in "largish"; use "fairly large."*)
jail	/dʒeɪl/	gaol
jailer	/ˈdʒeɪlə/	gaoler
janitor	/ˈdʒænɪtə/	caretaker, porter
Jell-O™	/ˈdʒɛloʊ/	jelly
jelly roll	/ˈdʒɛli ˌroʊl/	swiss roll
jersey (= *only for sports*)	/ˈdʒɜzi/	jersey (=*sweater*)
jeweler	/ˈdʒuələ/	jeweller
jewelry	/ˈdʒuəlri/	jewellery
jewelry box	/ˈdʒuəlri ˌbaks/	casket
to have a job		to be in work
❗ on the job (*This does not mean "having sex."*)		while working
join (*together*)	/dʒɔɪn/	join up
joint	/dʒɔɪnt/	join
jumper	/ˈdʒʌmpə/	pinafore
jump rope	/ˈdʒʌmp ˌroʊp/	skipping rope
kerosene	/ˈkɛrəˌsin/	paraffin
kind (*type*)	/kaɪnd/	sort
kindergarten	/ˈkɪndəˌgardən/	infant school
kneeled	/nild/	knelt
knobby	/ˈnabi/	knobbly
❗ knock someone up (*This does not mean "wake someone up."*)		to make a woman pregnant
know something by heart		know something off by heart
labeling	/ˈleɪbəlɪŋ/	labelling
laborer	/ˈleɪbərə/	labourer
ladybug	/ˈleɪdiˌbʌg/	ladybird
landing, boat landing	/ˈlændɪŋ/	quayside
last (*adv.*)	/læst/	lastly
latex paint	/ˈleɪtɛks ˈpeɪnt/	emulsion paint

U.S. Term	Pronunciation	British Equivalent
Laundromat	/ˈlɔndrəˌmæt/	launderette
laundry basket	/ˈlɔndri ˌbæskɪt/	linen basket, washing basket
laundry detergent	/ˈlɔndri dɪˈtɜrdʒənt/	washing powder
laundry (*clothes*)	/ˈlɔndri/	washing (*noun*)
lawyer (*in a court*)	/ˈlɔɪər/	barrister
lawyer (*outside a court*)		solicitor
layer cake	/ˈleɪər ˌkeɪk/	gateau, sandwich cake
lead pipe	/ˈlɛd ˈpaɪp/	lead piping
leaf through	/ˈlif ˈθru/	flick through
leaped	/lipt/	leapt
learned	/lɜrnd/	learnt
lease	/lis/	let
leash (*for dog*)	/liʃ/	lead
leasing agent	/ˈlisɪŋ ˌeɪdʒənt/	letting agent
left out (*forgotten*)		missed out
legal holiday	/ˈligəl ˈhɑlɪˌdeɪ/	bank holiday
lengthwise	/ˈlɛŋkθˌwaɪz/	lengthways, longways
letterhead	/ˈlɛtərˌhɛd/	headed paper
leukemia	/luˈkimiə/	leukaemia
license	/ˈlaɪsəns/	licence
license plate	/ˈlaɪsəns ˌpleɪt/	number plate
licorice	/ˈlɪkərɪʃ/	liquorice
lima bean	/ˈlaɪmə ˌbin/	broad bean
line (*noun*)	/laɪn/	queue
line up (*verb*); stand/wait in line	/laɪn ˈʌp/	queue up; queue
lineup	/ˈlaɪnˌʌp/	identification parade
liquor store	/ˈlɪkər ˌstɔr/	off licence
listen for		listen out for
liter	/ˈlitər/	litre
a little		a bit
little by little		bit by bit
liverwurst	/ˈlɪvərˌwɜrst/	liver sausage
living room	/ˈlɪvɪŋ ˌrum/	sitting room

U.S. Term	Pronunciation	British Equivalent
locks (*into something*)	/laks/	slots (*into something*)
log, logbook	/lɔg/, /'lɔg,bʊk/	log-book
loges	/'loʊʒɪz/	the sides of a dress circle
lollipop	/'lali,pap/	lolly
longhand	/'lɔŋ,hænd/	joined-up writing
longshore flow	/'lɔŋ ʃɔr 'floʊ/	longshore drift
longshoreman	/'lɔŋ'ʃɔrmən/	docker
look at		look over
lookout	/'lʊk,aʊt/	look-out
lose a turn		miss a go
be lost	/lɔst/	go missing
lost and found (department)	/'lɔst ən 'faʊnd/	lost property (office)
a lot of		lots of
lurking	/'lɜˑkɪŋ/	skulking
Ma'am	/mæm/	Madam
macaroni and cheese	/,mækə'roʊni ən 'tʃiz/	macaroni cheese
made of something	/meɪd/	made up of something
made to order		made to measure
magnifying glass	/'mægnə,faɪɪŋ glæs/	hand lens
mail (*verb, noun*)	/meɪl/	post
mailbox	/'meɪl,baks/	pillar box, postbox
mail slot	/'meɪl ,slat/	letter box
mail drop	/'meɪl ,drap/	pigeonhole
mailman, mail carrier	/'meɪl,mæn/, /'meɪl ,kæriəˑ/	postman
main article (*in a newspaper*)		leader
main street	/'meɪn ,strit/	high street
makeup	/'meɪk,ʌp/	make-up
maneuver	/mə'nuvəˑ/	manoeuvre
manure spreader	/mə'nur ,sprɛdəˑ/	muckspreader
mapmaking	/'mæp,meɪkɪŋ/	map-making
marmalade (*any kind of fruit jam*)	/'marmə,leɪd/	marmalade (*always made from citrus fruit*)
marquee (=*a sign or canopy over an entrance*)	/mar'ki/	marquee (=*a tent for an event*)

U.S. Term	Pronunciation	British Equivalent
marvelous	/'mɑrvələs/	marvellous
math	/mæθ/	maths
math problems		sums
mean (=unkind)	/min/	mean (=stingy, miserly)
measure (musical)	/'mɛʒɚ/	bar
measuring cup	/'mɛʒərɪŋ ˌkʌp/	measuring jug
meat/food grinder	/mit 'graɪndɚ/	mincer
meow	/mi'aʊ/	miaow
merry-go-round (carousel)	/'mɛri goʊ ˌraʊnd/	roundabout
mess (confusion)	/mɛs/	muddle
meter	/'mitɚ/	metre
mezzanine	/'mɛzəˌnin/	dress circle
midair	/mɪd'ɛr/	mid-air
midday	/'mɪd'deɪ/	mid-day
midwest(ern)	/ˌmɪd'wɛstɚn/	mid-west(ern)
military service	/'mɪlɪˌtɛri/	national service
milk delivery truck		milk float
milking shed	/'mɪlkɪŋ ʃɛd/	milking parlour
mimosa	/mɪ'moʊsə/	buck's fizz
mineral oil	/'mɪnərəl ˌɔɪl/	liquid paraffin
miss a turn		miss a go
be missing	/'mɪsɪŋ/	go missing
misspelled	/mɪs'spɛld/	misspelt
mixed up (confused)	/mɪkst/	muddled
mobile home	/'moʊbəl 'hoʊm/	caravan
modeling clay	/'mɑdəlɪŋ ˌkleɪ/	Plasticine™
molasses	/mə'læsɪz/	dark treacle
mold	/moʊld/	mould
moldy	/'moʊldi/	mouldy
mollusk	/'mɑləsk/	mollusc
molt	/moʊlt/	moult
Mom	/mɑm/	Mum
mononucleosis, mono	/ˌmɑnəˌnukli'oʊsɪs/	glandular fever
mouth guard	/'maʊθ ˌgɑrd/	gumshield
move around		move about

U.S. Term	Pronunciation	British Equivalent
movie theater	/'muvi ˌθiətə/	cinema
movie/film	/'muvi/	film
moving box		packing case
mug (a cup or someone's face)	/mʌg/	mug (also used to mean a "face")
muffler	/'mʌflə/	exhaust silencer
muscular	/'mʌskyələ/	muscly
music box		musical box
mustache	/'mʌstæʃ/	moustache
nabbed (arrested by police)	/næbd/	nicked
nail polish	/'neɪl ˌpɔlɪʃ/	nail varnish
named (a man named Richard)	/neɪmd/	called
nearby (town, city, etc.)	/'nɪr'baɪ/	neighbouring
nearby (close)		near by
neat	/nit/	tidy (adj.)
neaten	/'nitən/	tidy (verb)
neighbor	/'neɪbə/	neighbour
nervy	/'nɜvi/	cheeky
news clippings	/nuz klɪpɪŋz/	news cuttings
newsstand	/'nuzˌstænd/	bookstall, newsagent
newsstand	/'nuzˌstænd/	kiosk
next to last		last but one
nightstick	/'naɪtˌstɪk/	truncheon
nighttime, at night	/'naɪtˌtaɪm/	night-time
nipple (on a baby's bottle)	/'nɪpəl/	teat
No. 2 pencil		HB pencil
nonstop (continuous)	/'nan'stap/	non-stop
nontoxic	/'nan'taksɪk/	non-toxic
northeast(ern)	/ˌnɔrθ'ist/, /ˌnɔrθ'istɜn/	north-east(ern)
northwest(ern)	/ˌnɔrθ'wɛst/, /ˌnɔrθ'wɛstɜn/	north-west(ern)
note (write down)	/noʊt/	note down
nursery	/'nɜsəri/	garden centre
oatmeal	/'oʊtˌmil/	porridge, porridge oats

U.S. Term	Pronunciation	British Equivalent
ocean ("sea" is used less often)	/ˈoʊʃən/	sea
odometer	/oʊˈdɑmɪtɚ/	mileometer
office (doctor's, dentist's)	/ˈɔfɪs/	surgery
office building/tower		office block
once: (all) at once happen (only) once	/wʌns/	(all) in one go be a one-off; a one-off event
one-way ticket		single ticket
onto		on to
onward	/ˈɑnwɚd/	onwards
open-faced sandwich	/ˈoʊpən ˈfeɪst ˈsændwɪtʃ/	open sandwich
orangutan	/ɔˈræŋʊˌtæn/	orang-utan
orchestra (seats in a theater)	/ˈɔrkəstrə/	stalls
organize	/ˈɔrgəˌnaɪz/	organise
oriented	/ˈɔrientɪd/	orientated
outlet	/ˈaʊtlɛt/	power point
outside/outdoors	/ˌaʊtˈsaɪd/, /ˌaʊtˈdɔrz/	out of doors
outward	/ˈaʊtwɚd/	outwards
oven mitt	/ˈʌvən ˌmɪt/	oven glove
overalls	/ˈoʊvərˌɔlz/	dungarees
overflow (flood)	/ˌoʊvɚˈfloʊ/	burst banks
overpass	/ˈoʊvɚˌpæs/	flyover
overseas	/ˌoʊvɚˈsiz/	abroad
overtime	/ˈoʊvɚˌtaɪm/	extra time
pacifier (for a baby)	/ˈpæsəˌfaɪɚ/	dummy
package	/ˈpækɪdʒ/	parcel
package/pack	/ˈpækɪdʒ/, /ˈpæk/	packet
packet	/ˈpækɪt/	sachet
paddle, Ping-Pong™ paddle	/ˈpædəl/	bat, table tennis bat
pajamas	/pəˈdʒæməz/ /pəˈdʒaməz/	pyjamas
panties	/ˈpæntiz/	knickers
pantry	/ˈpæntri/	larder

U.S. Term	Pronunciation	British Equivalent
! pants (=*trousers*)	/pænts/	pants (=*underwear*)
pantyhose	/'pæntiˌhoʊz/	tights (*sheer*)
paper bag	/'peɪpɚ 'bæg/	paper carrier
paper cutter	/'peɪpɚ ˌkʌtɚ/	guillotine
paper towels	/'peɪpɚ 'taʊəlz/	kitchen paper
parakeet	/'pærəˌkit/	budgerigar
parentheses	/pə'rɛnθəsiz/	brackets
parka	/'parkə/	anorak
parking lot	/'parkɪŋ ˌlat/	car park
parlor	/'parlɚ/	parlour
part(s) (*piece*)	/part/	bit(s)
pass (*a car*)	/pæs/	overtake
pastry tube	/'peɪstri ˌtub/	icing bag
pavement (=*paving, tarmac*)	/'peɪvmənt/	pavement (=*sidewalk*)
paycheck	/'peɪˌtʃɛk/	wage packet
payroll clerk	/'peɪˌroʊl klɚk/	wages clerk
peanuts	/'piˌnʌts/	monkey nuts
! pecker (*DO NOT SAY "Keep your pecker up." Say, "Keep your chin up."*)	/'pɛkɚ/	penis
peddler	/'pɛdlɚ/	pedlar
! pee (*"Pee" is not a polite thing to say. Say "I have to go to the bathroom."*)	/pi/	wee
pen pal	/'pɛn ˌpæl/	pen-friend
percent	/pɚ'sɛnt/	per cent
period (*punctuation mark*)	/'pɪriəd/	full stop
person-to-person call	/'pɝsən tə 'pɝsən ˌkɔl/	personal call
p.e. stuff/clothes		kit
pharmacist	/'farməsɪst/	chemist
pharmacy	/'farməsi/	chemist's
phone booth	/'foʊn ˌbuθ/	call box
pickle	/'pɪkəl/	gherkin
pigs' feet		trotters
pimples	/'pɪmpəlz/	spots

U.S. Term	Pronunciation	British Equivalent
pinafore (=type of fancy apron with a bib)	/'pɪnəˌfɔr/	pinafore (=dress called a "jumper" in the U.S.)
! pissed (off) (slang)	/'pɪst 'ɔf/	angry
pit (in fruit)	/pɪt/	stone
pitcher	/'pɪtʃɚ/	jug
plaid	/plæd/	tartan
plane tickets	/pleɪn /	flight tickets
plastic bag	/'plæstɪk 'bæg/	carrier bag
plastic wrap (for food)	/'plæstɪk 'ræp/	clingfilm
play tag ("play catch" means to throw a ball back and forth)		play catch
Play-Doh™	/'pleɪˌdoʊ/	playdough
Plexiglas™ (clear acrylic resin)	/'plɛksɪˌglæs/	Perspex™
plow	/plaʊ/	plough
plug (verb)	/plʌg/	block up
plug (in a sink)		stopper
pocketbook (old-fashioned word)	/'pakɪtˌbʊk/	handbag
pocketknife	/'pakɪtˌnaɪf/	penknife
point (of a plan, activity, etc.)	/pɔɪnt/	aim
points (lose points for having done something)		marks
police officer	/pə'lis ˌəfəsɚ/	PC, WPC, constable
poncho (to wear in the rain)	/'pantʃoʊ/	cagoule
Popsicle™	/'papˌsɪkəl/	ice lolly
pot holder	/'patˌhoʊldɚ/	oven cloth
pour (verb)	/pɔr/	("tip" is never used to mean pour)
powdered sugar	/'paʊdɚd 'ʃʊgɚ/	icing sugar
practice (verb)	/'præktɪs/	practise
practice session (e.g., in a tennis game)	/'præktɪs 'sɛʃən/	knockabout
precinct (administrative territory)	/'prisɪŋkt/	district

U.S. Term	Pronunciation	British Equivalent
prenatal	/pri'neɪtəl/	antenatal
pretty	/'prɪti/	quite, rather, *or* very
president	/'prɛzɪdənt/	chairman
pressured (*environment*)	/'prɛʃəd/	pressurized
primary school	/'praɪmeri ˌskul/	junior school
produce	/'proʊdus/	fruit and vegetables
produce stand	/'proʊdus ˌstænd/	greengrocer
program (*not computer*)	/'proʊgræm/	programme
project, housing project	/'pradʒɛkt, 'haʊzɪŋ ˌpradʒɛkt/	council estate
propane bottle	/'proʊpeɪn ˌbatəl/	camping gas canister
propeller	/prə'pɛlər/	propellor
provide (*supply*)	/prə'vaɪd/	lay on
pry (*to open something*)	/praɪ/	prise
public school	/'pʌblɪk ˌskul/	state school
pulled up (*in a car*)		drew up
pump	/pʌmp/	court shoe
purebred	/'pyʊr'brɛd/	pure bred
purple (*Use "dark, brownish purple" instead of "puce."*)	/'pɝpəl/	puce
purse (=*handbag*)	/pɝs/	purse (=*wallet*)
pushcart	/'pʊʃˌkart/	barrow
pushpin (*molded top*)	/'pʊʃˌpɪn/	drawing pin
Q-tip®; swab	/'kyuˌtɪp ˌswab/	cotton bud
quarreling	/'kwɔrəlɪŋ/	quarrelling
quarter (*academic; 3 required in a year, 4th is optional*)	/'kwɔrtər/	term
quarter note	/'kwɔrtər ˌnoʊt/	crotchet
a quarter of/to/after (*the hour, as in "It's a quarter of seven."*)		quarter to/past (*"It's quarter to seven."*)
quite	/kwaɪt/	very
quotation marks	/kwoʊ'teɪʃən ˌmarks/	inverted commas
racetrack	/'reɪsˌtræk/	racecourse

U.S. Term	Pronunciation	British Equivalent
radio tube	/ˈreɪdioʊ ˌtub/	valve
raincoat	/ˈreɪnˌkoʊt/	mac, mackintosh, waterproof
rainforest	/ˈreɪnˌfɔrɪst/	rain forest
raise (*a child*)	/reɪz/	bring up, rear
raise (*in pay*)		rise
rappel	/ræˈpɛl/	abseil
rather	/ˈræðɚ/	very
red-handed	/ˈrɛd ˈhændɪd/	bang to rights
real (*for emphasis, as in "a real idiot"*)	/ˈriəl/	right
realize	/ˈriəˌlaɪz/	realise
Realtor™	/ˈriltɚ/	estate agent, letting agent
rearview mirror	/ˈrɪrvyu ˈmɪrɚ/	rear-view mirror
recess (*during school day*)	/ˈrɪsɛs/	break
received: was very well received	/rɪˈsivd/	went down a treat
record player	/ˈrɛkɚd ˌpleɪɚ/	gramophone
refrigerator (*"fridge" is used less*)	/rɪˈfrɪdʒəˌreɪtɚ/	fridge
refuses to listen		won't be told
relish	/ˈrɛlɪʃ/	pickle
rent (*something; only people are hired*)	/rɛnt/	hire
rent		let
rental car	/ˈrɛntəl ˌkar/	hire car
rented rooms		lodgings
reserve, make a reservation	/rɪˈzɜrv/, /ˌrɛzɚˈveɪʃən/	book (*verb*)
rest area (*roadside*)	/ˈrɛst ˌɛriə/	lay-by
restroom	/ˈrɛstˌrum/	WC, toilet, lavatory, cloakroom
resumé	/ˈrɛzuˌmeɪ/	CV, curriculum vitae
retainer (*on teeth*)	/rɪˈteɪnɚ/	brace
review (*for exams*)	/rɪˈvyu/	revise

U.S. Term	Pronunciation	British Equivalent
right:	/raɪt/	
right (*directly, e.g. right next door*)		bang (*e.g., bang next door*)
right after (*immediately after*)		straight after
right away (*immediately*)		straight away
get/do it right the first time		get it in one
right side up		right way up
river (*Used after the name, as in the Nile River.*)	/ˈrɪvɚ/	*Used before the name, as in the River Nile.*
road	/roʊd/	lane
roast	/roʊst/	joint (*of meat*)
robin (=*large red-breasted bird, symbol of spring*)	/ˈrabɪn/	robin (=*small red-breasted bird, symbol of Christmas*)
roller coaster	/ˈroʊlɚ ˌkoʊstɚ/	big dipper, roller-coaster
roof (*of car*)	/ruf/, /rʊf/	hood
roomer	/ˈrumɚ/	lodger
rooster	/ˈrustɚ/	cock, cockerel
ropes, tent ropes	/roʊp/	guy ropes
round trip ticket	/ˈraʊnd ˈtrɪp ˈtɪkɪt/	return ticket
route (*newspaper, mail carrier*)	/rut/, /raʊt/	round
rowboat	/ˈroʊˌboʊt/	rowing boat
!rubber	/ˈrʌbɚ/	condom (*Use "eraser" instead.*)
rubber band	/ˈrʌbɚ ˈbænd/	elastic band
rubber boots	/ˈrʌbɚ ˈbuts/	gum boots
rubbing alcohol	/ˈælkəˌhɔl/	surgical spirit
rummage sale	/ˈrʌmɪdʒ ˌseɪl/	jumble sale
rumor	/ˈrumɚ/	rumour
run (*in pantyhose*)	/rʌn/	ladder
run a red light		jump a red light
run by, run to (*a store, mall etc.*)		call in to
run down (*batteries*)		worn down
run for (*public office*)		stand for
run wild	/ˈrʌn ˈwaɪld/	run riot

U.S. Term	Pronunciation	British Equivalent
rutabaga	/ˌrutəˈbeɪgə/	swede
sack lunch	/sæk/	packed lunch
sacking	/ˈsækɪŋ/	sackcloth
safekeeping	/ˈseɪfˈkipɪŋ/	safe-keeping
sales clerk	/ˈseɪlz ˌklɝk/	shop assistant
saltine	/sɔlˈtin/	cream cracker
sand truck	/sænd trʌk/	gritter
sand (for roads)	/sænd/	grit
sanitation worker	/ˌsænɪˈteɪʃən ˈwɝkɚz/	dustman
Santa Claus	/ˈsæntə ˌklɔz/	Father Christmas
sausages	/ˈsɔsɪdʒɪz/	bangers
scallion	/ˈskælyən/	spring onion
schedule	/ˈskɛdʒul/	timetable
! scheme (=slightly dishonest plan)	/skim/	scheme (=any kind of plan)
(rounded/safety) scissors	/ˈsɪzɚz/	round-ended scissors
scold	/skoʊld/	tell off
Scotch tape™	/ˈskatʃ ˈteɪp/	Sellotape™
scrambled	/ˈskræmbəld/	clambered
scrapes	/skreɪps/	grazes
seafloor, seabed	/ˈsiˌflɔr/, /ˈsiˌbɛd/	sea-bed
search for (look for)	/sɝtʃ/	search out
seat belt	/ˈsit ˌbɛlt/	safety belt
second floor	/ˈsɛkənd ˈflɔr/	first floor
sedan (car)	/sɪˈdæn/	saloon
see if		check
seed (in fruit)	/sid/	pip
self-adhesive round labels		sticky spots
self-rising flour	/ˌsɛlf ˈraɪzɪŋ ˈflaʊr/	self-raising flour
semester (2 in a year)	/sɪˈmɛstɚ/	term (3 in a year)
semi, semitrailer	/ˈsɛmi/, /ˈsɛmaɪ/; /ˈsɛmiˌtreɪlɚ/	semi-articulated lorry
senior nurse	/ˈsinyɚ ˈnɝsɚ/	matron
service station	/ˈsɝvɪs ˈsteɪʃən/	petrol station
set the table		lay the table

U.S. Term	Pronunciation	British Equivalent
7-Up®	/'sevən 'ʌp/	lemonade
shade (window)	/ʃeɪd/	blind
sharp (about cheese)	/ʃarp/	aged
sharp (about how someone dresses)		smart
sharp (about how someone thinks)		quick-thinking and intelligent (this is not a negative word in the U.S.)
sheds	/ʃedz/	outbuildings
sheers	/ʃɪrz/	net curtains
sherbet (=sorbet with some milk in it)	/'ʃɚbɪt/	ice, sorbet
shifting gears	/ʃiftɪŋ/	going up/down a gear
shinbone	/'ʃɪn,boʊn/	shin-bone
shivering	/'ʃɪvərɪŋ/	shivery
shock absorbers	/'ʃak æb,zɔrbɚz/	dampers
shoelace	/'ʃu,leɪs/	lace
shopping bag	/'ʃapɪŋ ,bæg/	paper carrier, carrier bag
shopping cart	/'ʃapɪŋ ,kart/	shopping trolley
shot (injection)	/ʃat/	jab
shoulder (of a road)	/'ʃoʊldɚ/	verge
shoulder blade	/'ʃoʊldɚ ,bleɪd/	shoulder-blade
shredded coconut	/'ʃredɪd 'koʊkə,nʌt/	desiccated coconut
shrimp ("prawns" are only the very large ones)	/ʃrɪmp/	prawns
sick	/sɪk/	ill, unwell
get sick		fall ill
sidecar	/'saɪd,kar/	side-car
side mirror (on a car)	/'saɪd ,mɪrɚ/	wing mirror
sidesaddle	/'saɪd,sædəl/	side-saddle
sidewalk	/'saɪd,wɔk/	footpath, pavement
sideways to something	/'saɪd,weɪz/	sideways on to something
sift (verb); sifter (noun)	/sɪft/	sieve (verb, noun)
signal (motion)	/'sɪgnəl/	beckon
signal (in a car)		indicate
silly	/'sɪli/	jokey, daft

U.S. Term	Pronunciation	British Equivalent
sixteenth note	/ˈsɪksˈtinθ ˌnoʊt/	semiquaver
skateboard	/ˈskeɪtˌbɔrd/	skate-board
skeptical	/ˈskɛptɪkəl/	sceptical
skillet	/ˈskɪlɪt/	frying pan
skillful	/ˈskɪlfəl/	skilful
skycap	/ˈskaɪˌkæp/	airport porter
slacks	/slæks/	good trousers
the slammer (*jail*)	/ˈslæmɚ/	the nick
slap	/slæp/	smack
sled	/slɛd/	sledge
sleep in	/slip ɪn/	have a lie-in
sliced almonds	/ˈslaɪst ˈaməndz/	flaked almonds
slingshot	/ˈslɪŋˌʃɑt/	catapult (*handheld*)
slipcovers (*for furniture*)	/ˈslɪpˌkʌvɚz/	loose covers
slot machine	/slɑt məˌʃin/	fruit machine
small notebook	/ˈnoʊtˌbʊk/	jotter
smart	/smɑrt/	clever
smelled	/smɛld/	smelt
smoked herring	/smoʊkt/	kipper
smokestack (*industrial*)	/ˈsmoʊkˌstæk/	chimney
smooth (*verb*)	/smuð/	smooth off
snaps (*on clothes*)	/snæps/	press studs
snapshots	/ˈsnæpˌʃɑts/	snaps
sneakers	/ˈsnikɚz/	gym shoes, plimsolls
snow peas	/ˈsnoʊ ˌpiz/	mangetout
snowplow	/ˈsnoʊˌplaʊ/	snow plough
soccer	/ˈsɑkɚ/	football
soccer cleats	/ˈsɑkɚ ˌklits/	(football) boots
soccer players	/ˈsɑkɚ ˌpleɪɚz/	footballers
socket	/ˈsɑkɪt/	power point
soda cracker	/ˈsoʊdə ˌkrækɚ/	cream cracker
soft drinks	/ˈsɔft ˌdrɪŋk/	fizzy drinks
soil	/sɔɪl/	earth
somber	/ˈsɑmbɚ/	sombre
some (*drink, food*)	/sʌm/	a spot of (*something*)

S. Term	Pronunciation	British Equivalent
	/θroʊt/	gullet
g	/ˈθroʊ ˈʌp/	bring up, be sick
	/ˈθru.weɪ/	motorway
k (flat top)	/ˈθʌm.tæk/	drawing pin
g	/ˈθʌndərɪŋ/	thundery
	/ˌtɪk tæk ˈtoʊ/	noughts and crosses
	/ˈtɪd.bɪts/	titbits
paque)	/taɪts/	tights (=opaque or sheer)
O NOT use this ing someone.)	/ˈtɪŋkəl/	wee (urinate)
	/taɪrz/	tyres
	/ˈtɪʃu/	paper handkerchief
(bird)	/ˈtɪt.maʊs/	tit (as in blue tit or coal tit)
	/təˈdeɪ/	nowadays, these days
bject)	/ˈtɔɪlɪt/	toilet (=bathroom)
		sponge bag
twister	/tʌŋ/	tongue-twister
k	/ˈtuθ.pɪk/	cocktail stick
	/ˈtoʊtəli/	quite (=completely)
n a castle)	/ˈtaʊə/	keep
k	/ˈtoʊ ˌtrʌk/	breakdown truck
nd field)	/træk/	athletics
trailer rig/truck	/ˈtræktə/	articulated lorry
ircle	/ˈtræfɪk/	roundabout
ight/signal		traffic lights
	/ˈtreɪlə/	caravan
	/ˈtrænzɪt/	transport
on	/trænˈzɪʃən/	changeover
ission	/trænzˈmɪʃən/	gear box
ortation	/ˌtrænspəˈteɪʃən/	transport
	/træʃ/	rubbish
ag		bin liner
an		bin, dustbin
d	/ˈtrævəld/	travelled
er	/ˈtrævələ/	traveller

U.S. Term	Pronunciation	British Equivalent
somewhat	/ˈsʌmˌwʌt/	quite, rather
soprano recorder	/səˈprænoʊ rɪˈkɔrdə/	descant recorder
southeast(ern)	/ˌsaʊθˈistən/	south-east(ern)
southwest(ern)	/ˌsaʊθˈwestən/	south-west(ern)
spade	/speɪd/	trowel
spank (a child, on the bottom)	/spæŋk/	smack
spark plug	/ˈspark ˌplʌg/	sparking plug
sparkling (clean)	/ˈsparklɪŋ/	gleaming
spatula	/ˈspætʃələ/	fish slice
speak to someone	/spik/	have a word to someone
specially made/designed	/ˈspeʃəli ˈmeɪd/	purpose-built
specialty	/ˈspeʃəlti/	speciality
speed bumps	/ˈspid ˌbʌmps/	traffic calming scheme
spelled	/speld/	spelt
spilled	/spɪld/	spilt
spiraling	/ˈspaɪrəlɪŋ/	spiralling
splendor	/ˈsplendə/	splendour
split up	/splɪt/	hived off
spoiled	/spɔɪld/	spoilt
spool	/spul/	cotton reel
sporting goods store	/ˈsportɪŋ ˌgʊds/	sports shop
sports	/sports/	sport
sports complex	/sports ˈkampleks/	leisure centre
sprinkles	/ˈsprɪŋkəlz/	hundreds and thousands
Sprite®	/spraɪt/	lemonade
! spunk (=nerve, pluck); spunky (=plucky, spirited)	/spʌŋk/	spunk (=smegma); spunky (=full of smegma)
squash	/skwaʃ/	marrow
squished	/skwɪʃt/	squelched
squishy	/ˈskwɪʃi/	squidgy
staff (in music)	/stæf/	stave
standard	/ˈstændəd/	normal
get started	/startɪd/	off you go

U.S. Term	Pronunciation	British Equivalent
startle	/ˈstɑrtəl/	give someone a start
station wagon	/ˈsteɪʃən ˌwægən/	estate car
stay (on a path)	/steɪ/	keep (on a path)
steak sauce	/ˈsteɪk ˌsɔs/	brown sauce
steel wire	/ˈstil ˈwaɪr/	fuse wire
steel wool	/ˈstil ˈwʊl/	wire wool
stenciled	/ˈstɛnsəld/	stencilled
step on something		tread on something
(walking) stick		garden cane
sticky tack	/ˈstɪki ˌtæk/	Blu-tack™
stinger (on a bee)	/ˈstɪŋər/	sting
store ("shop"=small specialty store)	/stɔr/	shop
story (of a building)	/ˈstɔri/	storey
stove(top)	/ˈstoʊvˌtɑp/	cooker
straight (up) (alcoholic drink)	/streɪt/	neat
straighten up	/ˈstreɪtən/	tidy (verb)
strainer	/ˈstreɪnər/	sieve (noun)
strike (noun, verb)	/straɪk/	(take) industrial action
string bean	/ˈstrɪŋ ˌbin/	runner bean
strip (of bacon)	/strɪp/	rasher
striped	/straɪpt/	stripey
stroller	/ˈstroʊlər/	buggy, pushchair
struggle	/ˈstrʌgəl/	jostle
stuff (things in general)	/stʌf/	gear
! stuffed (="full of food" not "pregnant")	/stʌft/	full (up) (Americans do not say "get stuffed.")
styrofoam	/ˈstaɪrəˌfoʊm/	polystyrene
subdivision	/ˈsʌbdɪˌvɪʒən/	(housing) estate
subway (=underground train)	/ˈsʌbˌweɪ/	subway (=pedestrian underpass)
be a success	/səkˈsɛs/	go like a bomb
sucker (person)	/ˈsʌkər/	mug
sucker (thing)		lolly
suitcase	/ˈsutˌkeɪs/	case

U.S. Term	Pronunciation	British Equivalent
super (short for "supervisor")	/ˈsupər/	
superfine sugar/fine granulated sugar	/ˌsupərˈfaɪn ˈʃʊgər/	
supper	/ˈsʌpər/	
(office/art) supply store		
suspenders	/səˈspɛndərz/	
swap	/swap/	
sweater (jumper= pinafore dress)	/ˈswɛtər/	
sweatpants	/ˈswɛtˌpænts/	
sweatshirt	/ˈswɛtˌʃɜrt/	
swiveled	/ˈswɪvəld/	
tablespoon (measurement)	/ˈteɪbəlˌspun/	
tabouli	/ˌtəˈbuli/	
tag (on clothing)	/tæg/	
take care of		
take shelter		
take out (verb); takeout (noun) (food)	/ˈteɪkˌaʊt/	
tank (on a toilet)	/tæŋk/	
tape (adhesive)	/teɪp/	
tavern	/ˈtævərn/	
teakettle	/ˈtiˌkɛtəl/	
teammate	/ˈtimˌmeɪt/	
teaspoon (measurement)	/ˈtiˌspun/	
telephone pole	/ˈtɛləˌfoʊn/	
teller window (in a bank)	/ˈtɛlər ˌwɪndoʊ/	
tennis shoes	/ˈtɛnɪs ʃuz/	
test tube	/ˈtɛst ˌtub/	
theater	/ˈθiətər/	
Thermos™ (bottle)	/ˈθɜrməs/	
thighbone	/ˈθaɪˌboʊn/	
thoroughly	/ˈθɜrəli/	
thread	/θrɛd/	

U.S. Term	Pronunciation
throat	
throw up	
thruway	
thumbtack	
thunder	
tic-tac-toe	
tidbits	
tights (=	
! tinkle for ph	
tires	
tissue	
titmouse	
today	
toilet (=	
toilet b	
tongue	
toothp	
totally	
tower	
tow truck	
track	
tractor	
traffic	
traffic	
trailer	
trans	
trans	
trans	
trans	
trash	
trash	
trash	
travel	
travel	

U.S. Term	Pronunciation	British Equivalent
traveling	/'trævəlɪŋ/	travelling
triangle (*tool used for drawing*)	/'traɪˌæŋgəl/	set square
truck	/trʌk/	lorry
truck stop		lorry pull-in, transport café
trunk (*of car*)	/trʌŋk/	boot
try (*noun*): give something a try	/traɪ/	have a go
turn (*noun*):	/tɜn/	
turn (*direction, as in "first right turn"*)		turning
(it's your) turn		(it's your) go
take a turn		have a go
take turns		take it in turns
take turns throwing		take turns to throw
! tick off (=*make someone angry*)	/'tɪk 'ɔf/	tick off (=*check someone/something off a list*)
turnout (*roadside*)	/'tɜnˌaʊt/	lay-by
turn signal		indicator light
turpentine	/'tɜpənˌtaɪn/	white spirit
tuxedo	/tʌk'sidoʊ/	dinner jacket
type, types of	/taɪp/	sort, kinds of
UHT milk		long-life milk
underpants	/'ʌndəˌpænts/	(under)pants
undershirt	/'ʌndəˌʃɜt/	vest
underwear	/'ʌndəˌwɛr/	pants, knickers (*female*)
unraveled	/ʌn'rævəld/	unravelled
unused	/ʌn'yuzd/	disused
uppercase	/'ʌpəˈkeɪs/	capitals
upside down	/'ʌpsaɪd 'daʊn/	upside-down
upward	/'ʌpwəd/	upwards
vacation	/veɪ'keɪʃən/	holiday
vacuum cleaner	/'vækyum ˌklinə/	Hoover
vacuuming	/'vækyumɪŋ/	hoovering
valance (*on a curtain*)	/'væləns/	pelmet

WORD CONVERTER

U.S. Term	Pronunciation	British Equivalent
vanilla extract	/vəˈnɪlə/	vanilla essence
vapor	/ˈveɪpɚ/	vapour
vaudeville	/ˈvɔdvɪl/	music hall
vest	/vest/	waistcoat
vet (noun; the verb is not used much)	/vet/	veterinarian
veteran	/ˈvetərən/	ex-serviceman
visit (verb); visit (noun, verb)	/ˈvɪzɪt/	call on someone; chat
vomit	/ˈvɑmɪt/	bring up, be sick
wading	/ˈweɪdɪŋ/	paddling
wait around	/weɪt/	hang about
wait (on) tables		wait at tables
wakened	/ˈweɪkənd/	woken
walker	/ˈwɔkɚ/	Zimmer frame
walking shoe	/ˈwɔkɪŋ ʃu/	lace-up (shoe)
wall-to-wall carpet		fitted carpet
wander around	/ˈwɑndɚ/	wander about
warm up	/wɔrm/	knock-up (tennis)
warmer	/ˈwɔrmɚ/	less cold
wash: wash (yourself/someone) get washed up	/wɑʃ/	bath (verb) have a wash
washcloth	/ˈwɑʃˌklɔθ/	face cloth/flannel
wastebasket (for paper trash)	/ˈweɪstˌbæskɪt/	bin
watch, watch out for	/wɑtʃ/	mind (verb)
water heater	/ˈwɔtɚ ˌhitɚ/	immersion heater (electric)
waterline	/ˈwɔtɚˌlaɪn/	water-line
wax figure	/ˈwæks ˈfɪgyɚ/	waxwork
wax/waxed paper		greaseproof paper
Way to go!		Well done!
weather bureau	/ˈweðɚ ˌbyʊroʊ/	meteorological office
well-dressed		smart
while	/waɪl/	whilst
whine	/waɪn/	grizzle, whinge

U.S. Term	Pronunciation	British Equivalent
whole milk	/'hoʊl 'mɪlk/	full fat milk, full cream milk
whole note	/'hoʊl ˌnoʊt/	semibreve
whole wheat	/'hoʊl 'wit/	wholemeal
widthwise	/'wɪdθˌwaɪz/	widthways
wiggle	/'wɪgəl/	waggle
wildflower	/'waɪldˌflaʊɚ/	wild flower
Windbreaker™	/'wɪndˌbreɪkɚ/	wind cheater
windowsill	/'wɪndoʊˌsɪl/	window-sill
windshield	/'wɪndˌʃild/	windscreen
with or without milk/cream		black or white coffee/tea
witness stand	/'wɪtnɪs ˌstænd/	witness box
woolen	/'wʊlən/	woollen
wool hat		bobble hat
workers	/'wɚkɚz/	workmen
workout stuff/clothes	/'wɚkˌaʊt ˌstʌf/ /'wɚkˌaʊt ˌkloʊz/	kit
worn	/'wɔrn/	tatty
worshiped, worshiping	/'wɚʃɪpt/, /'wɚʃɪpɪŋ/	worshipped, worshipping
wrench	/rɛntʃ/	spanner
an X		a cross
yarn	/'yɑrn/	wool (spun)
yogurt	/'yougɚt/	yoghurt
yogurt container	/'yougɚt kənˌteɪnɚ/	yoghurt pot
yummy	/'yʌmi/	scrummy
zero	/'zɪroʊ/	nought, O
zip code	/'zɪp ˌkoʊd/	postcode
zipper	/'zɪpɚ/	zip
zits (slang)	/zɪts/	spots
zookeeper	/'zuˌkipɚ/	zoo-keeper
zucchini	/zu'kini/	courgettes

IN THE KNOW IN THE U.S.A.

In the Know in the U.S.A. is an indispensable guide for businesspeople and their families to adapt to life in the United States. More than just a list of dos and don'ts, *In the Know* provides a thorough understanding of the culture, explains proper social etiquette, describes the business environment, and provides essential reference information for the whole family.

EASY PRONUNCIATION

Improve your American English pronunciation with the simplest, most practical audio program available! Includes six 60-minute CDs and a 64-page reference guide.